Education Empire

SUNY series, Educational Leadership
Daniel L. Duke, editor

Education Empire

The Evolution of an Excellent Suburban School System

Daniel L. Duke

State University of New York Press

Published by
State University of New York Press, Albany

For information, address State University of New York Press,
194 Washington Avenue, Suite 305, Albany, NY 12210-2365

Production by Diane Geneles
Marketing by Anne M. Valentine

Library of Congress Cataloging-in-Publication Data

Duke, Daniel Linden.
    Education empire : the evolution of an excellent suburban school
    system / Daniel L. Duke.
        p. cm. — (SUNY series, educational leadership)
    Includes bibliographical references and index.
    ISBN 0–7914–6493–8 (hardcover : alk paper) — ISBN 0–7914–6494–6
    (pbk. : alk. paper)
    1. Fairfax County Public Schools—History—Case studies. 2. Suburban
schools—Virginia—Fairfax County—Case studies. 3. School management
and organization—Virginia—Fairfax County—Case studies. I. Title. II.
Series: SUNY series in educational leadership.

LD7501.F14D85 2005
3709′.9755′291—dc22
                                                                    200401833

10 9 8 7 6 5 4 3 2 1

Dedicated to the thousands of committed educators and educational leaders who have made Fairfax County Public Schools a beacon of hope for school systems across the nation

Contents

Illustrations

Tables

Preface

In the fall of 1997 President Clinton told his commission on U.S. race relations that Fairfax County would be a good place to study how people from different backgrounds live, work, and go to school together (Lipton and Benning, 1997). His observation confirmed a suspicion of mine that more attention should be devoted to understanding what goes on in suburbs and suburban school systems. Researchers in education are captivated by the complexity of urban schooling and the nostalgic innocence of rural schooling, but the fact remains that a majority of American youth grow up and attend school in suburbs. President Clinton singled out Fairfax County because it is increasingly characterized by the diversity—cultural, linguistic, religious, and socioeconomic—that once was associated exclusively with cities. To understand America's future, it is essential that we understand what is happening to its suburbs and school systems.

My effort to advance this understanding focuses on one Virginia school system—Fairfax County Public Schools—during the tumultuous years from 1954 to 2004. This half century witnessed unprecedented growth in Fairfax County and its schools, the Brown decision and desegregation, the expansion of state and federal governments' roles in local education, the influx of large numbers of poor and non-English-speaking students, the advent of elected school boards, and the institution of sweeping accountability measures. In order to become the highly acclaimed school system that it is today, Fairfax County Public Schools had to confront all of these challenges and more.

The title's reference to Fairfax County Public Schools as an *education empire* is not intended as an attention-grabbing gimmick. One of the nation's largest school systems, Fairfax serves roughly one out of every seven students in Virginia—over 166,000 students as of 2004. In addition, the school system runs extensive programs for preschool-age youngsters with special needs and adults seeking to earn a G.E.D. or simply expand their knowledge.

In 2003 the school system's Office of Adult and Community Education recorded a total enrollment of 84,519 in its courses, making it the largest adult education operation in the nation. To see that students get to school and back, the school system operates one of the largest bus fleets in the United States. Each school day 1,500 buses transport 110,000 students to and from schools. Fairfax's food services unit provides meals for 145,000 students and staff members each school day. In addition, senior citizens were served more than 97,000 meals at 23 school sites in 2003. With over 21,000 employees, Fairfax County Public Schools (FCPS) is one of Virginia's largest employers. The continuing education of this massive workforce is yet another of the school system's responsibilities. In 2002–2003, almost 9,000 teachers took courses offered by the FCPS Academy.

While no one would argue that Fairfax is a *typical* suburban school system, it has faced and is facing a number of challenges— such as population growth and increasing numbers of students from poor and culturally and linguistically diverse families—that are likely to confront other suburban school systems over the coming years. More importantly, Fairfax has been able to address these challenges without experiencing a dramatic decline in educational excellence. The giant school system, in fact, has actually continued to raise student achievement, in the process demonstrating that there is good reason to be hopeful regarding the prospects for public education.

My fascination with Fairfax County Public Schools began when my program area at the University of Virginia's Curry School of Education established an off-grounds degree program for prospective school administrators in Northern Virginia. I was impressed with the intelligence and commitment of the Fairfax educators who took my courses. As they completed projects related to the history and operation of Fairfax County Public Schools, I began to acquire a basic understanding of the forces shaping this remarkable school system. I have drawn heavily on the fine work of these graduate students and would like to express my appreciation to Patricia Addison, Brenda Aiken, Pam Ballato, Denny Berry, Mark Boyd, Jeff Carroll, Martha Chamberlin, Jonathan Chang, Jamie Deaton, Kim Dockery, Elizabeth Duckworth, Esther Eacho, Sharon Eisenberg, Amy Goodloe, Karen Sue Hurwitz, Erin Jones, Denise Katz, Angela Kheradmand, Kathleen R. Lamont, Joanne Leone, Yvette Lewis, Melony Mackin, Jamilla Mannie, Jay McClain, Linda R. Mezera, Phyllis Pajardo, Shelley Prince, Alice

Reilly, David Spage, and Grace Wang. My graduate research assistant, Mason Miller, deserves special recognition for his efforts to locate primary resource material and dissertations related to Fairfax County Public Schools.

A round of thanks also must be extended to a number of individuals who are or have been associated with Fairfax County Public Schools and who provided invaluable insights during formal interviews. These individuals include Sylvia Auton, Ray Diroll, Michael Eckhoff, John English, Robert E. Frye, Michael Glascoe, James Johnson, Alan Leis, Kitty Porterfield, Maryanne Roesch, Nancy Sprague, Jane Strauss, and Gayle S. Wood. Donna Tait, Fairfax's Teleproductions Manager, was kind enough to share videotapes on the history of the county school system. The staff of the Virginia Room at the Fairfax Public Library were immensely helpful in locating back issues of local newspapers and school district publications and reports. Jessica Foster of the FCPS Professional Library provided access to a variety of key documents and enormous encouragement to complete the project. Special commendation is due the Metro section of *The Washington Post*, which for decades has provided consistent and balanced coverage of education news in Northern Virginia.

Introduction

The Promised Land is changing. The ultimate destination for generations of hardworking citizens—the American suburb—is experiencing shifts of tectonic proportions. Tranquil subdivisions are being displaced by high density housing. Traffic congestion in the suburbs now rivals or exceeds that of urban areas. Crime and poverty also have moved to the suburbs. Once the proud bastion of white America, the suburbs increasingly attract residents representing diverse races, cultures, and languages. A central assumption of this book is that the sweeping changes washing over suburbia can be understood better by examining changes in suburban education.

I shall focus on one suburban area—Fairfax County, Virginia—and its school system—Fairfax County Public Schools or FCPS. Fairfax County, of course, is not just any suburban area. It is one of, if not the wealthiest counties in the United States. Strategically located across the Potomac River from Washington, D.C., the 399-square-mile county is home to over a million residents. The school system that serves Fairfax County is no ordinary school system either. As of 2004, FCPS was the nation's 12th largest school district, with over 166,000 students and an annual budget of over $1.5 billion. Thirteen percent of all students in Virginia are enrolled in the 241 schools and centers of FCPS. The organizational structure of the district, which employs more than 21,000 professional and nonprofessional workers, is comparable to that of a Fortune 500 company.

When considering Fairfax County and its school system, it is tempting to dwell on size, but there is more to the story than big enrollments and big budgets. Fairfax County is also the land of big

1

expectations. What makes FCPS such a fascinating focus for inquiry has been the school system's ability, year in and year out, to meet many of these big expectations. FCPS has changed over the years to meet the changing needs of its population and shifting economic and political circumstances without diminishing its reputation for educational excellence. Unlike many once-great school systems, FCPS has eschewed complacency and refused to rest on its laurels. The story of Fairfax County Public Schools, while certainly not an educational fairy tale, is a chronicle of continuing commitment to quality education for all students.

Over most of the last half century, Fairfax has graduated an impressive percentage of its students and sent a substantial number of them on to higher education, often at some of the nation's leading colleges and universities. The school system's flagship magnet school—Thomas Jefferson High School for Science and Technology—is arguably the top high school in the United States. Thomas Jefferson administers more Advanced Placement tests than any other high school and boasts an outstanding record for scholarships and academic awards. It is one type of accomplishment for a single school to achieve success and quite another for an entire school system to do so. When that school system includes 241 schools and centers, and 91 percent of them are meeting or exceeding state accreditation standards—a 70 percent pass rate in various subjects among all students in each school—the achievement is truly remarkable (Helderman and Keating, 2002). The handful of schools that are not meeting standards are targeted for special assistance and allocated additional resources. The district's handbook for 2003-2004 proudly noted the following achievements:

- 90 percent of high school graduates continue on to some form of postsecondary education.
- The dropout rate for FY 2001 fell to 1.9 percent, lower than the averages for Virginia and for the nation.
- FCPS seniors who took the SAT in 2002 had an average combined score of 1,096. This far exceeds the average combined scores of 1,016 in Virginia and 1,020 in the nation.
- 95 percent of FCPS special education program students were working or attending school or both six to nine months following graduation.
- In FY 2000, 67.6 percent of graduates earned advanced diplomas.

Fairfax's track record of success is a major reason for its choice as the focus of this book. A strong case can be made, in fact, that

Fairfax County Public Schools is the best school system in the nation. When Fairfax hired a consulting firm in the late nineties to study exemplary school systems and identify benchmarks that could be used in guiding improvement efforts, the consultants reported that they had difficulty completing their assignment. In their field work they discovered that FCPS was the benchmark against which other exemplary school systems measured themselves!

A second reason for examining FCPS is the county's status as a bellwether for suburban America. The seismic forces currently reshaping Fairfax County and its schools eventually will ripple across other suburbs. Understanding how FCPS has been able to address these forces and maintain or, in many cases, improve the quality of its programs may provide important information for policymakers and educators.

The Evolution of an Empire

An enterprise as vast as Fairfax County Public Schools cannot easily be placed under a microscope. A wide-angle lens is more appropriate for studying such a school system's evolution. Comprehensiveness and detail must give way to parsimony and selectivity if a half century's organizational history is to be condensed into one volume.

The approach that I chose for conducting this study was developed and refined in a previous project that resulted in the 60-year history of Thomas Jefferson High School in Richmond, Virginia (Duke, 1995). Referred to as *organizational history*, the approach combines the historian's concern for continuity and change with the sociologist's interest in the forces that shape institutions. Like most complex bureaucratic organizations, large school systems such as Fairfax typically hunger for stability. Periodically, however, despite their best efforts, school systems are buffeted by the winds of change. On occasion, pressure for change even may build from forces within the school system. In an organizational history, the researcher makes every effort to identify both external and internal pressures for change and to understand how and why the school system responded as it did to these pressures. Organizational historians assume that a range of choices is possible whenever pressures for change arise. Depending on circumstances, school systems may opt to embrace, ignore, resist, or subvert change. Why particular choices are made at particular points in a school system's history becomes a central focus for inquiry.

What makes the organizational historian's task especially challenging is the fact that pressures for change often travel in packs. At the same time that Fairfax faced court-ordered desegregation, it also had to address exploding enrollments. A decade later, enrollments fell off, presenting new problems. Simultaneously, the economy suffered a downturn, thereby amplifying the need for retrenchment. Fast forward another decade, and the nation demanded greater educational excellence from all schools, so that it could compete in an increasingly global economy. At the same time, local pressure grew for greater attention to the needs of at-risk students. Accounts that analyze how a school district has addressed one particular challenge, such as diversity or inadequate resources, sometimes fail to capture the complexity of operating today's systems, where solitary challenges are rare. The goal of the present history is to examine the impact of multiple pressures for change on the evolution of an outstanding suburban school system.

Contemporary organization theorists refer to large and complex operations like Fairfax County Public Schools as *open systems* (Scott, 1992). Open systems interact on a continuing basis with their environments. These environments, in the case of a school system, range from local neighborhoods to regional partnerships to state and federal governments. While open systems have boundaries, it is not always easy to determine the lines separating them from their various environments. Buckley (1967) pointed out that the interactions between open systems and environments are of two basic kinds—(1) those aimed at preserving or maintaining the status quo and (2) those intended to change the status quo. The history of Fairfax County Public Schools includes examples of both types of interactions. In some instances, the school system's desire for change has been moderated by environmental pressure for stability. In other cases, the impetus for change derived from environmental forces, and the school system balked. There also have been occasions when both the school system and the environment agreed that it was necessary to initiate or resist change.

In order to make sense of the give-and-take relations between Fairfax and its environment, a political perspective is necessary. "From a political perspective," according to Bolman and Deal (1997, p. 175), "organizational goals, structure, and policies emerge from an ongoing process of bargaining and negotiation among major interest groups." These groups are found within as well as outside organizations. A political perspective assumes that groups often are characterized by "enduring differences" in "values, beliefs, information, interests, and perceptions of reality" (Bolman and Deal, 1997, p. 163). An additional assumption is that resources are always limited. The combination of enduring differences between groups and limited resources means that the potential for conflict is ever present. The evolution of Fairfax County Public Schools is a chronicle of competition among a variety of stakeholder groups regarding the allocation of resources for education.

Much of this book focuses on decisions that have been instrumental in defining the "character" of Fairfax County Public Schools and the services it provides. Because it is impossible to cover every key decision over a half century, the account focuses on particular types of decisions, including decisions dealing with the organizational structure of the school system, enrollment changes, district leadership, public accountability, and certain instructional challenges, including minority student achievement, the education of immigrants, special education, and gifted and talented education.

The first two chapters of the book look at Fairfax County Public Schools from 1954, when the Supreme Court rendered its momentous decision in *Brown vs. Board of Education of Topeka* and the first baby boomers began to arrive at the doorsteps of Fairfax elementary schools, until 1984. This latter date provides a convenient dividing point for several reasons. By the early '80s, as students around the United States boarded the train bound for educational excellence, many Fairfax County students already were well down the line. By 1984 FCPS had achieved a reputation as a high-performing school system. Not all Fairfax students, of course, shared in their school system's success. In 1984 FCPS launched a major initiative to address the needs of poor and minority students. One in every 10 Fairfax students by this time was foreign born, a figure that would steadily climb over the ensuing years. Other reasons why 1984 constitutes a useful watershed include the fact that the period of enrollment decline that reached back into the '70s came to an end, marking the beginning of a new era of rapid growth, and the school system's financial picture brightened appreciably after years of tight money and budget squabbles. Finally, Fairfax embarked on a search for a new Superintendent in 1984, a search that would bring Boston's Robert R. Spillane to Northern Virginia the following year.

The next four chapters cover the period from 1985 to 2004, during which Fairfax County Public Schools demonstrated its ability to sustain and, in some cases, expand its educational achievements. Maintaining a record of accomplishment in a stable environment is one thing; it is quite another to do so amidst turbulence. The two decades from 1984 to 2004 were anything but tranquil for FCPS. First, the period was marked by an unprecedented influx of new students, representing diverse language, cultural, and religious groups. The percentage of students receiving free and reduced-price lunch rose, as poverty migrated from the cities to the suburbs. In the midst of its efforts to address the concerns of an increasingly needy student population, Fairfax experienced three dramatic changes. For the first time in November of 1995, school board members in Fairfax County were elected by popular vote. Previously they had been appointed by the Fairfax County Board of Supervisors. What had once been a modestly political process overnight grew into an intensely partisan business. Adding to the politicization of education, not only in Fairfax but across Virginia, was the advent of a statewide educational accountability initiative that included Standards of Learning, high-stakes tests on the standards, new Standards of Accreditation with sanctions for low-performing schools, and School Performance Report Cards that allowed parents and the media to compare student performance across schools. As if these major changes weren't enough, the decade-long prosperity "bubble" burst in 2000. Fairfax County, with its abundance of high-tech firms and upscale commercial operations, found itself facing substantial revenue problems. The departure of Robert Spillane and the hiring of New York's Daniel Domenech in 1997 added a new ingredient to the simmering mixture.

Chapter 3 looks at Fairfax's efforts to handle renewed enrollment growth while simultaneously accommodating an unprecedented increase in student diversity. Special attention is devoted to the lingering achievement gap between white and minority students and the measures taken by the school system to reduce it. Chapter 4 zeroes in on the intensification of educational politics in Fairfax County, a process that culminated in the switch to elected school boards. To illustrate the heightened politicization of educational decision making, the chapter discusses Fairfax's attempt to implement merit pay and the school system's seesaw battles over sex education. Chapter 5 examines how FCPS has dealt with contemporary pressures for greater educational accountability, in particular Virginia's Standards of Learning and the federal No Child Left Behind Act. In order to handle the myriad of challenges that have faced and still confront Fairfax

County Public Schools, the school system has continually refined its organizational structure. Chapter 6 focuses on the organization of FCPS, especially its central administration, and how the huge school system handles certain critical functions such as quality control and leadership development.

The concluding chapter of *Education Empire* reflects on the recent history of Fairfax County Public Schools in an attempt to understand the problems and possibilities that lie ahead for suburban school systems. Lessons are drawn from Fairfax's efforts to address growth and diversity without sacrificing high performance. Such lessons could hold the key to success for the next generation of suburban schools.

Multiple Data Sources—The Key to Organizational History

Chronicling the history of a complex enterprise like Fairfax County Public Schools requires the collection and verification of a considerable body of data. No single source of information is sufficient. Tapping multiple data sources helps to separate the incontestable *facts* from matters of opinion and controversy. In order to tell the story of Fairfax County Public Schools over the last half century, it was necessary to review local newspapers, including the *Fairfax Herald*, the *Fairfax Journal*, and the *Northern Virginia Journal*, and the Metro section of *The Washington Post*, which covers major educational developments in the vicinity of the nation's capital. Together with annual reports prepared by the Superintendent for the Fairfax School Board and School Board minutes, these data sources were used to construct a basic chronology of events in the school system's history from 1954 to 2004. Additional details that might not appear on a journalist's radar screen or in the Superintendent's annual report and board minutes were gathered in interviews with key informants—mostly individuals with lengthy experience in FCPS and a broad perspective on its operations. Documents produced by FCPS, including committee reports and commissioned studies, along with case studies of various units of the school system that were compiled by graduate students enrolled in the University of Virginia's advanced degree programs in northern Virginia, offered still more information of historical value.

The next step in the research leading up to this book called for identifying *critical incidents*, points at which the school system faced serious challenges and pressures for change. Since it is impossible to record everything that happens over 50 years in a school system as large as FCPS, these critical incidents served as useful foci for discussion and analysis. Faced with a particular challenge or a set of challenges, what options were considered by district leaders? Why were particular options ruled out? Why were other options embraced? These questions require the organizational historian to move from description to explanation and interpretation. Explaining why a school system opts for one direction rather than another is not as clear-cut a process as identifying critical incidents. Explanations can vary, depending on the perspective of the observer. Where the reasons for a particular course of action were unclear, key informants provided valuable insights to help in interpreting data. Other useful information came from dissertations conducted on various aspects of the Fairfax school system.

Had FCPS not been a school system that valued self-study, the task of compiling this history would have been much more difficult. Great school systems do not shy away from inquiries into their performance and how to improve it. Access to data from internal studies and reports offered a wealth of statistical and interpretive data that otherwise might have been unavailable to the author. No Fairfax educator with whom an interview was requested ever refused their cooperation, testimony to the fact that the spirit of inquiry is alive and well in Fairfax County.

In the account to follow, readers hopefully will come to appreciate the tremendous complexity and daunting challenges facing contemporary suburban educators. There are few tasks in today's society that are any more difficult or more critical to the future than managing the education of a community's young people. Just because the *community* is an affluent suburb is no reason to assume that the task is any simpler or easier.

CHAPTER 1

A Classroom a Day

A latter-day Rip Van Winkle who fell asleep in Fairfax County in 1954 and woke up 20 years later would have found it hard to believe he was in the same place. A review of the county's schools and enrollment figures provides an explanation. In 1954 FCPS had 42 elementary schools and 6 high schools. The school division operated two systems, one for white students and one for African-American students. Six of the elementary schools and one of the high schools served African-American students. The one black high school, Luther Jackson, had just opened in 1954. Previously, African-American students from Fairfax County who desired a high school education had to commute to a vocational training center in Manassas, Virginia, or cross the Potomac River to attend a Washington, D.C. high school. Enrollment figures for Fairfax students ages 6 through 19 totaled 14,652, with half of this number consisting of students between 6 and 9 years of age (*Annual Report of the Superintendent of Public Instruction...*, 1953–54, pp. 242–243). Roughly 8 percent of the total enrollment were African-American students.

By 1974 the number of schools serving the youth of Fairfax County had climbed to 168, including 18 high schools, 18 intermediate schools, and 4 combined high school/intermediate schools. Enrollment had skyrocketed to 136,508 students, over 9 times the number of students 20 years earlier. African-American and white students no longer attended separate schools. At the height of the construction program required to keep pace with this rapid growth, Fairfax was erecting the equivalent of a classroom a day.

It is tempting to focus the story of Fairfax County Public Schools and its rise to educational prominence on enrollment growth and school construction. There is much more to the story, however. In the midst of a mushrooming school population, FCPS

9

had to confront the challenge of desegregation and state-sanctioned defiance of the U.S. Supreme Court. Close on the heels of desegregation came the Elementary and Secondary Education Act of 1965 with its emphasis on meeting the educational needs of students from disadvantaged backgrounds. No longer would the federal government's role in local education be a minor one. As Fairfax County Public Schools grew, organizational adjustments were necessitated. A Superintendent and small central office staff might have been able to oversee the operation of 48 schools, but not four times that number.

Chapter 1 covers the history of FCPS from 1954 until 1976, when school enrollments began to fall. The opening section looks at the school system's efforts to contend with surging enrollments during the '50s and early '60s. Subsequent sections address Fairfax's response to court-ordered desegregation, a process that consumed the entire decade following the *Brown* decision; the expanding educational role of the federal government and its impact on Fairfax; the proliferation of programs designed to meet the special needs of different groups of students; and Fairfax's growing interest in educational innovation and reorganization. The chapter closes with signs in the early '70s that two decades of growth and progress were coming to an end. The school system had demonstrated its ability to cope successfully with growing enrollments, desegregation, and pressures to address special needs. Whether it could preserve gains in the face of retrenchment remained to be seen.

Boomers by the Bushel

Schools are built to accommodate a certain number of students. When enrollments grow so rapidly that new schools cannot be built fast enough, school capacities are quickly exceeded, creating conditions that can foster a variety of problems, including overcrowded classrooms and corridors, increased behavior problems, reduced curriculum choice, and diminished instructional effectiveness. To avoid these problems, school systems try to estimate population growth and complete the construction of new facilities *before* existing facilities burst at the seams. Despite its best efforts, FCPS, like many school systems in the '50s and '60s, found it almost impossible to keep up with the pace of growth. Mary Musick (1999), a veteran of almost half a century with FCPS,

KEY DATES FOR FAIRFAX COUNTY PUBLIC SCHOOLS: 1954–1975

1954 U.S. Supreme Court strikes down school segregation in Brown v Board of Education of Topeka

FCPS opens its first secondary school for African-American students

1955 Superintendent W. T. Woodson distributes first manual containing standard administrative practices

1956 Doctrine of "massive resistance" initiated by Virginia General Assembly

1958 FCPS School Board votes to switch from 7-5 to 6-2-4 grade-level configuration

1959 FCPS becomes the second Virginia jurisdiction to adopt a voluntary desegregation plan

1960 FCPS schools officially desegregate (freedom of choice plan)

1961 W. T. Woodson retires and is replaced by E. C. Funderburk

1964 FCPS opens its first elementary center for gifted students

1965 FCPS drafts plan to close remaining all-black schools

Congress passes Elementary and Secondary Education Act

FCPS receives Head Start funding

1966 FCPS enrollment surpasses 100,000

Adult Education Program begins

1967 FCPS receives federal grant to launch Center for Effecting Educational Change

FCPS begins to reorganize into "areas"

1968 Half-day kindergartens begin

1970 S. John Davis becomes Superintendent

1971 FCPS begins work on system-wide curriculum guidelines and objectives (Program of Studies)

1972 Virginia implements the Standards of Quality for all public schools

1974 In Lau v. Nichols, U.S. Supreme Court determines that school systems must provide special assistance to non-English-speaking students

FCPS launches its first English as a Second Language program

FCPS develops tests aligned to Program of Studies

1975 Congress passes PL 94-142, the Education of the Handicapped Act

recalled teachers having to conduct lessons on the auditorium stage or in windowless closets due to lack of instructional space.

Fortunately for the young people of Fairfax County and their teachers, local taxpayers displayed a willingness to support the expansion of school facilities. Many of these taxpayers were recent arrivals, having been drawn to the mostly rural county by war-related employment opportunities. Following World War II and the Korean Conflict, a large number of these individuals elected to remain in the Washington suburbs and raise families. The National Broadcasting Company (NBC), according to the official history of Fairfax County (Netherton, et al., 1978, pp. 577-578), "chose the county to serve as an example of county-financed school expansion in a series of ten broadcasts on matters regarding the nation's public schools in November 1955." To accommodate the 238 percent increase in school enrollment between 1951 and 1961, Fairfax taxpayers supported $69,500,000 in bonded indebtedness (Netherton, et al., 1978, p. 577). It helped that a high percentage of Fairfax's population was 19 or younger and, therefore, in need of educational services. In 1950 roughly 38 percent of Fairfax residents were under 20 (Netherton, et al., 1978, p. 703). A decade later the percentage had soared to almost 45 percent. It was hard to find a Fairfax taxpayer who did not have at least one child and, consequently, a pressing reason to support the public schools.

As school enrollments climbed and new schools opened, the ranks of Fairfax educators swelled. Table 1.1 shows the total number of instructional positions, including supervisors, principals, head teachers, and teachers, in 1953-54, 1959-60, and 1963-64.

Table 1.1
Total Instructional Positions (Supervisors, Principals,
Head Teachers, and Teachers) for Fairfax County
Public Schools in 1953-54, 1959-60, and 1963-64

	WHITE			AFRICAN-AMERICAN			TOTAL
	Male	Female	Total	Male	Female	Total	
1953-54	134.5	714.5	849	6	37.5	43.5	892.5
1959-60	495.67	1,651	2,146.67	21	75	96	2,242.67
1963-64	877.8	2,463.8	3,341.6	25.5	73.2	98.7	3,440.3

Statistics are derived from the *Annual Reports of the Superintendent of Public Instruction of the Commonwealth of Virginia* for 1953-54, 1959-60, and 1963-64.

Supervisors, principals, and head teachers accounted for 6 percent of the total instructional positions in 1953-54 and 1959-60, but the percentage dropped to 5.8 by 1963-64. The average teacher salary steadily rose over this period, from $3,693 in 1953-54 to $5,109 in 1959-60 to $6,575 in 1963-64. Vocational education teachers earned the highest salaries, followed by high school and then elementary schoolteachers.

Overseeing the operation of Fairfax County Public Schools during the baby boomer '50s was a central administration that seems skeletal in comparison with later years. It is important to remember, however, that this period predated the advent of federal and state legislation aimed at creating programs for students with special needs and the extension of school-based services to the community. In 1954 the central administration of FCPS consisted of the division Superintendent, W. T. Woodson, and the following positions:

  Assistant Superintendent
  Administrative Assistant
  Director, Building and Grounds
  Director, Maintenance
  Director, Personnel
  Director, Surveys and Information
  Clerk of School Board and Finance Officer
  Supervisor of Transportation
  Supervisors of Cafeterias
  Attendance Officers (3)

In addition to these positions, the central administration included a Department of Instruction with 26 professionals. These individuals were distributed as follows:

  Director of Instruction
  Supervisors of Secondary Schools (2)
  Supervisors of Elementary Schools (4)
  Supervisor of Negro Elementary Schools
  Supervisor of Speech Education
  Helping Teachers in Music (2)
  Helping Teacher in Art
  Chairman of Helping Teachers in Reading
  Helping Teachers in Reading (4)
  Visiting Teachers (6)
  Coordinator of Special Education and Juvenile Workers
  Psychologist
  Film Librarian

Superintendent Woodson recognized that the growth in enrollments, schools, and instructional staff required a measure of stan-

dardization that had been unnecessary previously. Toward this
end, he issued an *Administrative Guide for Fairfax County Schools*
in August of 1955. The handbook was intended for principals, the
first effort to formalize expectations for Fairfax building leaders.
In his foreword, Woodson acknowledged that the school system
was entering a new era: "As our school system has grown and our
operations have become increasingly complex, the need for stan-
dardizing our practices and procedures within the framework of
adopted policy and such rules, regulations, and laws as may apply
becomes more apparent."

Developed by a committee consisting of three principals, a
teacher, two supervisors, and two members of the Superintendent's administrative staff, the handbook represented a compila-
tion of a quarter century's policies and practices for operating
schools. Duties for all central office administrators were spelled
out, as was the role of principals. With regard to the latter group,
the handbook noted that,

> The principal is in direct control of the program of his
> school and is responsible to the Superintendent, through
> his staff assistants, for the proper performance of his
> duties. As the person responsible for the school and its pro-
> gram, it follows that everything that goes on in a school
> must be under his supervision and cognizance. Instruction,
> in-service training, supervision of instruction, special or
> extra-curricular activities, custodial and maintenance
> work, building and equipment care and use by school and
> non-school groups, business and accounting, provision for
> supplies, discipline of pupils, and the entire field of public
> relations are the responsibility of each school principal,
> and must be under his control and cognizance. (p. 2)

Several pages later the handbook specified additional responsibilities for principals. These included how to deal with salesmen
and visitors, fund-raising drives, maintaining pupil records, and,
in a sign of the times, overcrowding. The last duty included the following provisions:

> In the event of serious overcrowding, half-day shifts or use
> of temporary classroom space may be resorted to. It is the
> policy of the School Board to employ double shifts in

grades one and two rather than rent classroom space away
from the school ... (p. 4)

Those familiar with contemporary expectations for principals
will notice the absence of references to leadership, instructional
leadership, leadership for change, or school improvement. The
principal of the '50s, at least in Fairfax County, was an "organization man," to use the term made famous by William H. Whyte. He
was expected to be a manager, not a change agent. Seeing that
policies and regulations were enforced was valued far more than
initiative and innovation.

In the *Superintendent's Annual Report* for 1956-57, Woodson
spelled out the school system's mission:

The objectives of the public schools of Fairfax County are to
promote and develop in each pupil basic knowledges, skills and
understandings which enable him:

> To speak with understanding
> To speak fluently and correctly
> To write with clarity
> To perform with accuracy the basic mathematical pro-
>   cesses and use them properly
> To search for knowledge effectively
> To reason and analyze
> To know his abilities, capacities and interests
> To know and understand the world around him
> To develop and maintain sound mental and physical
>   health
> To know and appreciate the past

Perhaps more noteworthy than these objectives was the
report's tone, which foreshadowed the school system's future
emphasis on a high quality academic program and exceptional student achievement. Parents of first, second, and third graders, for
example, were informed that their children would spend more
than 400 hours, or an average of over two hours daily, in the study
of reading, writing, and arithmetic. Older elementary students
would average two-and-a-half hours each day. Meanwhile, students in need of assistance could expect to receive help from a
reading specialist, be assigned to a "low mental group," or attend a
special summer school. The performance of Fairfax students on the

Stanford Achievement Tests (grades 4 and 7) and the Iowa Silent Reading Tests (grades 7 and 8) exceeded national norms in all areas except arithmetic reasoning (where Fairfax students *only* equaled national norms). The report boasted that half of Fairfax's high school graduates in 1957 planned to attend college.[1] Woodson proudly reported that 85 percent of Fairfax's teaching staff held college degrees, including 16 percent with master's degrees.

In one area, however, Superintendent Woodson could not be boastful. Try as it might, FCPS's capital improvement program could not keep pace with population growth. When the fall semester began in 1958, Fairfax High School, built to accommodate 1,000 students, was stuffed with 2,100 students ("Fairfax High School...," *Fairfax Herald*, September 5, 1958, p. 1). Principal Coffey was forced to make arrangements to bus 529 eighth graders to Jermantown School for half their classes and lunch. Overcrowding confronted other Fairfax schools and would continue to do so for years to come.

In the midst of coping with surging enrollments, the Fairfax School Board decided to abandon the system's 7-5 format in favor of a 6-2-4 grade-level configuration ("6–2–4 Plan...," *Fairfax Herald*, July 25, 1958, p. 1). Instead of students attending elementary school for seven years and high school for five years, they would spend six years in elementary school, two years in intermediate school, and four years in high school. Eighth-grade work would continue to be counted toward high school graduation, a provision that was set by the Virginia Board of Education. In order to alter its grade-level organization, FCPS needed to launch a massive building program. Eight new intermediate schools opened in the fall of 1960 to inaugurate the new arrangement. Each of the million-dollar facilities consisted of 40 classrooms, including 6 science laboratories, 2 art laboratories, 2 homemaking rooms, and 2 industrial arts shops, plus a library, gymnasium, cafeteria, guidance rooms, and space for band, chorus, and health instruction. By 1964 Fairfax's school ranks swelled to 15 intermediate schools. Launching the 6-2-4 plan was W. T. Woodson's last major initiative as Superintendent.

An era came to an end when Woodson retired in 1961, after serving as Superintendent for 32 years. The only Superintendents Fairfax had known since 1886 were Woodson and his predecessor, Milton D. Hall, who served for 43 years. Their successors would spend far less time atop the school system's swelling bureaucracy. Woodson stepped down just as Fairfax County and the state of Virginia were compelled to face the consequences of the Brown decision.

Delayed Desegregation

By the time the Supreme Court handed down its ruling in *Brown v. Board of Education of Topeka*, Fairfax County was well on its way to completing construction of Luther P. Jackson High School, the county's first high school for black students.[2] No longer would black students desiring postelementary schooling have to make arrangements to attend segregated Manassas Regional High School, a vocational training center in Prince William County, or travel across the Potomac River to one of several Washington, D.C. high schools available to black students. When Jackson first opened on September 1, 1954, it included elementary as well as high school classes in order to take maximum advantage of available space. Enrollment growth was challenging black as well as white elementary facilities. Black parents who had lobbied for years to get their own high school under the dual system of separate schools for blacks and whites must have been struck by the ironic timing of Luther Jackson's opening.

In November of 1954 the Fairfax School Board received a letter from the Women's Club of Franklin Park urging the creation of a committee to study the effect of desegregation on Fairfax school children (Lee, 1993, p. 74). At the same time the Board also received a petition signed by 80 county residents requesting a "smooth changeover from segregated to non-segregated schools" (Lee, 1993, p. 74). The School Board President indicated that the Board was unprepared to act on either suggestion. Years would pass before decisions regarding implementation of the Brown decision were handled by individual school systems in the Commonwealth.

Virginia's political and educational leaders may have extolled the virtues of local control of education, but when the U.S. Supreme Court declared segregated schooling to be unconstitutional in 1954, they had no intention of leaving the decision of whether or not to desegregate to localities. The official position, one that eventually would lead to the doctrine of massive resistance, began to take shape in the *Annual Report of the Superintendent of Public Instruction* for 1953-1954. Published soon after the Brown decision, the report opened with reference to "a new challenge":

As the 1953-54 Report goes to the printer the citizens of Virginia are faced with the impact of a Supreme Court

decision handed down on May 17, 1954, declaring unconstitutional the plan of segregated schools in operation in
Virginia with public funds for nearly eighty-five years. The
separate but equal doctrine was prescribed by the
Supreme Court in 1896...

The Court has asked specifically for advice on whether it
should permit gradual adjustment or should order Negro
children admitted immediately to schools of their choice
within normal district lines...

A brief has been submitted to the Court stating that an
indefinite period of time for adjustment to its anti-segrega-
tion ruling must be granted if public education in any form
is to survive in Virginia.

It has been pointed out that government still derives its
foundation from the consent of the governed and that
custom, beliefs, and feelings of individuals cannot be legis-
lated, nor can a Court decree or executive order force a
result basically contrary to the wishes of a people.

A sharp contrast to this declaration, attorneys representing the Negro have urged the Court to order an end to
racial segregation as promptly as administrative changes
can be made. (pp. 25-26)

Whether local school systems such as Fairfax County, left to
their own, would have moved forward to implement desegregation
in the late fifties will never be known. Richmond removed any possibility of local option, when members of Virginia's General
Assembly, with the strong support of U.S. Senator Harry F. Byrd,
adopted a series of bills in August and September of 1956 that
came to be known as the Stanley Plan.[3] The cornerstone of the
massive resistance doctrine, the Stanley Plan called for the creation of a statewide Pupil Placement Board. All local requests for
student transfers between schools had to be handled by this central board. It soon became clear that the chief purpose of the Pupil
Placement Board was to preserve segregation. To their credit, leg-
islators from Northern Virginia went on record opposing the
Stanley Plan and massive resistance (Ely, 1976). Along with many
business leaders, they urged Governor J. Lindsay Almond to con-
vene a special session of the General Assembly to repeal the measures. Their pleas went unheeded.

Meanwhile black students across Virginia began to petition for transfers to white schools, citing the closer proximity of white schools to their homes and inequities between the programs and resources available in black and white schools. When 22 black students from Warren County had their petitions rejected by the Pupil Placement Board, they sought redress from the courts and won. Under court order to desegregate, Warren County became the first jurisdiction in Virginia to shut down its public schools rather than comply. In the fall of 1959, a year after Warren County's dramatic action, 26 black students from Fairfax County petitioned the School Board to be transferred to white schools. The School Board rejected three of the requests on technicalities and forwarded the other 23 requests without recommendation to Richmond ("Pupil Placement Unit Rejects All Requests for School Transfers," *The Washington Post*, August 4, 1959, p. B-1). The Pupil Placement Board rejected all 23 petitions along with every petition from other jurisdictions. By this time, however, Virginia's brief flirtation with civil disobedience was coming to an end. Both the Virginia Supreme Court and federal district court had declared school closings intended to prevent integration to be unconstitutional. Two weeks after these rulings, on February 2, 1959, 21 black students entered previously all-white schools in Norfolk and Arlington (Pratt, 1992, p. 11). Desegregation at both locations occurred without incident.

On August 8, 1959, Fairfax County became the second jurisdiction in Virginia to adopt a voluntary plan for desegregating its schools. Only Arlington had preceded it, but its 1956 plan had been scuttled, when Virginia opted for massive resistance. Drafted in closed sessions by the School Board, the details of the Fairfax desegregation plan were not immediately made public. The plan was rumored to call for a gradual approach, beginning with the integration of first grade in the fall of 1960 and continuing with an additional grade each year until all 12 grades were integrated (McBee, 1959). Frustrated over the secrecy surrounding the School Board's plan, lawyers for the 26 black students who earlier had their petitions for transfer denied brought suit in federal district court to immediately attend all-white schools in Fairfax County.

Adopting the secret plan for desegregation did not prevent the Fairfax County School Board from continuing to support segregationist policies. Superintendent Woodson sent a memo to all high school principals informing them that, in light of House Joint Resolution 57, no Virginia school could participate in athletic events against teams that included both whites and blacks. Also in accordance with state policy, the School Board mailed out tuition grant applications in August of 1959 to parents who did not want their child to attend an integrated school. The *Fairfax Herald* ("School Board Integration Plan....," August 21, 1959) reported that more than 100 requests for the $250 grants were received. The grants could be used at any public or private nonsectarian school.

On September 22, 1960, Federal Judge Albert V. Bryan issued a court order for Fairfax County Public Schools to admit some of the 26 black students to previously all-white schools, thereby initiating the process of desegregation in Fairfax County. For the next five years, FCPS followed a gradualist policy referred to as "freedom of choice." Under this arrangement, the burden for seeking transfers to white schools was placed on black parents. Requests for transfer were not always granted, and black parents complained about unnecessary red tape and arbitrary denials (Lee, 1993, p. 76). Black parents, for example, were required to measure the distance between their residence and the nearest black and white schools in order to prove that the white school was closer. Initially, if a transfer request was granted, the black student's parents had to provide transportation to the white school.

By the fall of 1962, 214 black students were enrolled in previously all-white schools in Fairfax County. In March of the following year, the School Board received a report indicating that more than a million dollars in construction costs could be saved by abolishing its dual system of schools ("Dual School Setup Hit as Costly," *The Washington Post*, March 31, 1963). All-black schools at this point were not filled to capacity. Allison W. Brown Jr., chairman of the schools committee of the County Council on Human Relations and the author of the report, put his argument thusly:

> Since, of the 73,000 children in County schools, only 2200 or about 3 percent, are in Negro schools, it is obvious that residents of the County are allowing themselves a substantial extravagance by keeping these 2200 Negro children in segregated schools.

The demise of the dual system of schools in Fairfax County would take another three years, additional litigation, and a court order from the Fourth Circuit Court of Appeals. In 1965 the School Board adopted a three-stage process for closing the remaining all-black schools or converting them to integrated schools. The U.S. Commissioner of Education certified in April of 1965 that Fairfax County Public Schools was in compliance with the Civil Rights Act of 1964. Despite years of foot dragging on the road to desegregation, Fairfax County could boast that it was among the first school systems in the nation to receive the Commissioner's certification (Eacho, 2001).

Fairfax and the Feds

Today it is easy to forget that the federal government's active role in public education is a relatively recent development. Prior to the sixties, the primary link between Washington and Fairfax County Public Schools involved impact aid. Public Law 815 and Public Law 874, both passed in 1950, assisted local school systems with substantial numbers of federal employees, including military families, by providing financial assistance for school construction and operation. In the 1953-54 school year, for example, FCPS received $764,200 from the federal government to assist in school construction and a total of $1,468,128 in federal aid (*Annual Report of the Superintendent of Public Instruction...*, 1953-54, p. 194).

In April of 1965, a new era of federal involvement in education began with the passage of the Elementary and Secondary Education Act (ESEA). President Lyndon Johnson hailed the bill, predicting that "this is just the beginning, the first giant stride toward full educational opportunity for all of our school children" (Carper, 1965). Since 1965 billions of federal dollars have been allocated to school systems across the United States to support the various titled programs of the ESEA. Fairfax County's share of the funds has been substantial.

Because Fairfax County responded more rapidly than other school systems in Virginia to the requirement for an approved desegregation plan, it qualified immediately for the funds provided under the ESEA. Other school systems in Virginia had to wait to apply for federal assistance until their desegregation plans could be drafted, submitted, and approved. The major component of the ESEA was Title I, which allocated millions of dollars annually to raise the quality of education for poor children. The bill originally earmarked $349,000 for Fairfax, based on the number of students from families earning $2,000 or less a year.

The formula subsequently was changed to include families on welfare, thereby increasing the allocation for which Fairfax qualified.

Less than a week before the U.S. Senate approved the ESEA, Fairfax County learned that it would be one of the first school systems in the nation to receive a federal grant under the Civil Rights Act to aid school desegregation (Grant, 1965). The $54,000, along with additional local funds, were used to finance inservice training for teachers, a summer workshop, speech classes, and improved guidance services. Inservice training familiarized teachers with different language patterns among white and black students, introduced strategies for communicating effectively, and helped teachers analyze their own communications. Home economics teachers attended a one-day summer workshop on personal care and grooming, presumably so they could assist students involved in desegregation ("A Guide to Intergroup Education," 1965, p. 7). Staff development also aimed to help teachers "discuss the abilities of Negro students, maintenance of school standards, curriculum adjustments and ways to encourage student acceptance of members of other races" (Grant, 1965). The school system's application for federal funding noted that the advent of full desegregation meant that for the first time white teachers would be working in previously all-black schools under black principals and vice versa.

The spring of 1965 also found Fairfax County receiving its first Head Start funds. When Congress passed the Economic Opportunity Act (Public Law 88-452) in 1964, it approved federal support for child care centers as a weapon in the War on Poverty. In February of the next year the first lady officially launched Project Head Start. Aware of a growing number of poor families, FCPS already had initiated pilot child care projects in three "culturally disadvantaged areas" (Larson-Crowther, 1966). With federal funds available to support an expansion of child care services, the school system quickly prepared proposals for full-year and summer Head Start programs. The summer program proposal was approved on May 15, 1965, thereby enabling 24 centers serving 686 preschool-age children to operate for six weeks. On September 30, 1965, the proposal for full-year programs received the green light, allowing 24 full-day and 2 half-day child care centers to join the existing pilot programs. The regular school-year programs enrolled 716 children in their first year. Of these, 659 came from disadvantaged backgrounds (Larson-Crowther, 1966, p. 8). The 7 goals of Fairfax's Head Start programs included the following (Larson-Crowther, 1966, p. 2):

1. To raise the children's level of aspiration.
2. To help them to develop into happy, well-adjusted, socially responsible children.
3. The development of improved communicative skills by the children.
4. The promotion of better health among the children.
5. The encouragement of better attitudes by the parents toward the educational attainment of their children.
6. The development of teacher understanding and respect for under-privileged children.
7. The development of neighborhood and community concern for the underprivileged child.

The War on Poverty helped sensitize suburban communities like Fairfax to the fact that privation was not just an urban and rural problem. Amidst its growing affluence, Fairfax was home to a substantial number of poor families. In 1959 Fairfax had 4,534 families (7.7%) earning under $4,000 annually (Netherton, et al., 1978, p. 706). A decade later the number had risen to 5,103, though the percentage had dropped to 4.5 percent. Fairfax was gaining well-to-do families at a much faster rate than poor families, a fact that would foster the illusion for the uninformed that Fairfax had no poverty problem. The School Board acknowledged that the county had an obligation to address the special needs of the poor, when it responded to a study of poverty in Fairfax at its February 4, 1974, meeting (School Board Agenda Item IV-A, February 4, 1974). Conducted by the Anti-Poverty Commission of Fairfax, the study noted that the plight of the county's poor had been investigated a number of times, but little of consequence had resulted. A "countywide definitive plan for groping with the problems caused by poverty of the underachiever, the under-motivated" was recommended to replace the existing collection of "separate and distinct programs having no overall plan for coordination."

Fairfax County Public Schools again benefited from the new federal commitment to public education when, on July 27, 1967, a Title III (ESEA) grant of $396,000 was received to establish the Center for Effecting Educational Change (CEEC). Premised on the belief that most of the problems faced by the school system were "too complex for one individual's competence," the center was structured to facilitate a team approach to problem solving and planning (Proposal for the Operation of a Center for Effecting Educational Change, January 12, 1967). The four primary purposes of the

CEEC were (1) to study and research the change process itself, (2) to develop and initiate a systematic change procedure, (3) to provide special services, including assistance to teachers in promoting change, and (4) to serve as an exemplary center. Among the CEEC's initial activities were studies of pilot kindergarten classes at 7 elementary schools, performing arts in Fairfax schools, and the needs of students with "special learning problems." One Fairfax educator recalled the CEEC's invaluable assistance in moving her elementary school from its traditional "self-contained" instructional model to a more up-to-date format characterized by cooperative teaching, family-type groupings, miniclasses, and learning centers (Musick, 1999). Among its services to the school, the CEEC solicited input from parents regarding the instructional improvement initiative. With the creation of the CEEC, FCPS's commitment to cutting-edge innovation was firmly established. That commitment has remained strong ever since.

A day after learning of its federal grant for the CEEC, FCPS was informed that it had been chosen to administer a $97,000 grant for Fairfax, Arlington, and Alexandria to set up the Center for Adult Basic Education Learning (CABEL). The center's mission included the creation of adult basic education materials, the demonstration of new instructional techniques for adult basic education, and the evaluation of adult basic education programs. At this time Fairfax was serving over 16,000 adult learners each year.

By the late sixties, Fairfax's education empire was alive and well. From preschool child care centers to adult basic education, there was hardly any age-group or aspect of educational service in which the district was uninvolved. The school system's elementary and secondary enrollment passed 100,000 in 1966, and the numbers would continue to climb, though not as dramatically as during the preceding decade, for another 10 years. In addition to well-to-do newcomers seeking the privileges of suburbia, Fairfax attracted a number of nontraditional pilgrims, including the poor and the culturally diverse. Spurred by the availability of surging local revenue and ample federal aid to education, FCPS expanded the number of programs designed to address the special needs of various groups of students.

Program Proliferation

America's educational gift to the world presumably is the common school, an institution where, as the name implies, all stu-

dents regardless of family circumstances receive the same education. As Fairfax County and other school systems began to confront growing student diversity in the mid-'60s, they realized that
the basic academic program needed to be supplemented, if the
needs of different types of students were to be addressed effectively. Public education was not well served by a "one size fits all"
mentality. In his annual report for 1964-1965, Superintendent E.
C. Funderburk, who succeeded W. T. Woodson in 1961, signaled
the new era by noting the range of new initiatives being introduced in Fairfax schools. Programs for gifted students were
started in elementary schools, pilot programs for preschoolers from
poor families were launched, and vocational education to prevent
students from dropping out was expanded. In 1968 FCPS launched
a county-wide kindergarten program.

Programs for gifted students

Concern that American schools were not doing enough to culti-
vate their most talented students surfaced in the wake of the
Soviet Union's successful launch of Sputnik on October 4, 1957.
Fears arose that America was falling behind the U.S.S.R. in the
preparation of scientists and mathematicians. In order to promote
academic excellence, reformers urged the development of honors
and Advanced Placement courses. Calls for the consolidation of
small high schools were prompted by a desire to attain enrollments sufficiently large to sustain special tracks for the brightest
students (Conant, 1959, pp. 77–85). Highly acclaimed scientists
became involved in projects to develop state-of-the-art curricula for
high school students.

Located in the shadow of the nation's capital and populated by
a large number of government and military officials, Fairfax
County could not escape pressure to develop programs geared to
the needs of gifted young people. Advanced Placement courses
were introduced in the late '50s. In the fall of 1964, FCPS opened
its first elementary centers for "superior learners" (Lamont, 2002;
McClain, 2001). A total of 35 students, all in grades 4 through 6
and with IQs of 140 or higher, participated in the initial program,
co-located at Bailey's and Hollin Hills Elementary Schools.
Students were drawn from all parts of the county. Parents had to
provide transportation to the half-day, self-contained centers.

Perhaps because of the egalitarian spirit of the '60s or the fact
that the concerns of policymakers had shifted to promoting equal
educational opportunity, Fairfax's gifted program grew slowly over

the next few years. By 1967 only 108 students in grades 3 through 6 were participating in self-contained classes for "superior learners" at 6 elementary schools. The school system, however, had assumed responsibility for transporting gifted students to their programs. The purpose and design of the gifted program was laid out in a 1967 report, "Programs for the Gifted Child." A gifted student was defined as a young person in the top 1.5 percent of the population in intellectual ability as measured by an individual intelligence (IQ) test.

Gifted education was expanded to include two intermediate schools (Kilmer and Mark Twain) in 1969. Unlike the elementary centers, the intermediate program focused on specific subjects. In 1970 eighth graders who were judged to be gifted in mathematics were allowed to take algebra. Soon the demand for gifted offerings compelled the school system to provide programs at every intermediate school.

As the gifted program expanded, parents of gifted students began to exert more influence (Lamont, 2002). In a paper submitted to district officials in 1970 they lobbied for a program director and secure funding. They also indicated that only a quarter to a third of the eligible students in Fairfax were being served. Complaints were expressed regarding irregularities in the identification of eligible students. The paper addressed the two primary options for delivering gifted education—center-based programs and enrichment opportunities provided at each child's neighborhood school. Parents came down decidedly in favor of center-based programs:

> A small minority of educators suggests that the regular elementary school can meet the needs of gifted children through acceleration and enrichment. The consensus of experts in education of the gifted, however, is that such a program slights the emotional needs of the child without adequately meeting his intellectual needs.... We know from our own experience the loneliness and boredom of our children before they entered the County program.... We are convinced that the problems created by grouping our children—transportation time and removal from their immediate neighborhoods—are more than outweighed by the benefits of the special class. ("Strengthening the Fairfax County Program of Education for Gifted Children," April 9, 1970)

Following the report from parents regarding their desires for gifted education, FCPS conducted an evaluation of its offerings. The evaluation found that the more established programs functioned more effectively than the newer programs. When the possibility of expanding gifted education into high school was investigated, it was determined that high schools already provided gifted students with sufficient opportunities for advanced work. All that was needed, the evaluation concluded, were better mechanisms for directing gifted students to the most challenging courses. The evaluation also suggested that a program director was needed to advocate for resources, coordinate activities, and plan staff development of gifted education teachers.

The federal government began to play a more assertive role in gifted education in the early '70s. As a result of a congressional mandate to study the needs of gifted students and determine how the federal government should be involved in gifted education, a large study was conducted. The findings appeared in 1972 in a report titled *Education of the Gifted and Talented*. The report recommended that gifted education be better regulated and that terminology and procedures be standardized. A federal Office of Education for the Gifted and Talented was established, and a government-sponsored clearinghouse for information on gifted and talented programs was located in Reston (Fairfax County). In response to the federal initiative, FCPS promulgated standardized screening and identification procedures, developed a district plan, and created an advisory committee for gifted and talented students (Lamont, 2002).

Close on the heels of federal efforts to promote gifted education were initiatives from Richmond. When the General Assembly approved a set of Standards of Quality (SOQ) in 1972 to guide Virginia school systems, it endorsed a provision for special education that called for the identification of gifted students and the development of appropriate educational opportunities for them (McClain, 2001). When the SOQ were updated in 1973, school systems were required to provide special services designed to enrich the educational experiences of gifted and talented students. The following year the General Assembly appropriated $30 per student, up to a total of 3 percent of each school system's student population, to support gifted and talented programs.

Federal and state efforts played a pivotal role in the expansion of services for gifted students in Fairfax. By 1973 FCPS had extended full-time gifted education to students in grades 3 through 8. Participation in center-based programs rose to 454 students.

Targeted interventions

Many of Fairfax's gifted students would have succeeded in school even if special programs had not been made available. Other students, however, required targeted assistance if they were to stand a reasonable chance of benefiting from their schooling. FCPS had long recognized the individual needs of low-achieving students, but it was not until the late '60s that the range of interventions available to them broadened. As noted earlier, much of the impetus for expanded services derived from the unprecedented availability of federal funds.

In the '50s, when Fairfax students experienced academic difficulties, there were three basic options other than dropping out of school. They could receive assistance from a small cadre of specialists, including special education teachers, helping teachers in reading, helping teachers in speech, visiting teachers who worked "with the school, home, and community to discover and eliminate causes which may prevent boys and girls from making satisfactory achievement in school," and homebound teachers for students with physical disabilities. According to the *Superintendent's Annual Report* for 1956-1957, 897 students (2.4%) received special assistance in reading and 180 students (.5%) were placed in "low mental groups." Students also could attend remedial summer school programs. In 1956-1957, 171 elementary students received remedial reading help, 60 elementary students received remedial mathematics help, and 697 secondary students re-took courses in which they had not performed well.

The third option for Fairfax students who struggled academically was to enter a nonacademic diploma track. The choices in the '50s included a commercial, a vocational, and an elective track. Regardless of the track, students had to fulfill the state's graduation requirements, which included 4 years of English and 1 year each of science, mathematics, U.S. and Virginia history, and U.S. and Virginia government (for a total of 8 credits). In addition, Fairfax County Public Schools required students earning an academic diploma to take an additional year of social studies and an additional year and a half of mathematics. Students working in the other tracks also needed a year of social studies, but they were required to take only two semesters (rather than three) of mathematics.

With the advent in the mid-'60s of federal legislation and funding aimed at providing equal educational opportunity for all students, the focus of assistance expanded to include early childhood education and new instructional programs. The *Superintendent's Annual Report* for 1964-1965, for example, cited three pilot programs:

1. Classes for the "Culturally Different": These classes include the precursors to Head Start preschool classes as well as Head Start classes.

2. Classes for "Highly Gifted" Children.

3. Extended learning time: Algebra I was expanded from a one to a two-year course for "below average" students. FCPS sought to determine whether this arrangement was preferable to assigning less able students to general mathematics.

In addition, FCPS expanded its training centers for special education students to accommodate 120 students (up from 70 the previous year) and created a pilot program for mildly mentally handicapped boys at Edison High School. Six additional classes for boys were scheduled to begin in the fall of 1965 with newly acquired federal funds. Superintendent Funderburk noted that 2,300 elementary students received special instruction in reading, though he pointed out that another 400 students were on a waiting list to receive supplementary services. Almost 15 percent of all Fairfax high school students were involved in some form of vocational education.

As enrollments climbed, the number of students receiving special education services grew, though perhaps not as much as one might imagine. By the standards of the post-Public Law 94-142 (1975) era, when school systems often identified 10 percent or more of their students as eligible for special education, Fairfax in the early '70s served relatively few disabled students. Of 135,839 students in 1973-1974, 2,103 (1.6%) were involved in special education (Eacho, 2001). Furthermore, there was little evidence of the diversity that would lead to a variety of targeted interventions in the decades to come. In 1973-1974, blacks represented the largest minority group in Fairfax with 3.4 percent, followed by Hispanic Americans (.7%), Asian Americans (.6%), and Native Americans (.05%).

Despite their relatively small numbers, students from other cultures were not overlooked by Fairfax County Public Schools. As early as 1965, Superintendent Funderburk, in his annual report, recognized teachers' need for professional development related to other cultures:

In years ahead we need to step-up the professional growth and development of the entire staff as well as continue to develop and make use of new teaching materials, different approaches to teaching, emphasis not only on our own culture and heritage, but also on the teaching of the cultures of Central America, South America, and the Far and Near East—(It is imperative that we learn as much as possible of the culture of those people whose ideologies are different from ours but with whom we must learn to communicate and live.)

He could not have known that by 2001, 31 percent of Fairfax residents would live in a household where English was not spoken (Whoriskey and Cohen, 2001). Of the 226,800 foreign-born Fairfax residents in 2001, half came from Asia and 31 percent from Latin America.

On July 27, 1973, the School Board approved a new policy intended to sensitize schools to non-Christian religions and religious holidays. The policy, which at least one board member feared would spawn lawsuits, allowed each of the county's 169 schools to determine if and how it would observe religious holidays (Whitaker, 1973). Principals were directed to appoint a committee "to review and guide the school's thinking, planning, and implementation of educational programs relative to religion and religious holidays." The following year FCPS initiated its first English as a Second Language (ESL) programs. The 375 students initially involved in ESL tended to be well-educated children from diplomatic corps families (Eacho, 2001). By 1976 ESL programs had skyrocketed to 2,800 students. The impetus for ESL programs was the U.S. Supreme Court's decision in *Lau v. Nichols* in 1974. As a result of the case, which involved the claim that the San Francisco school system had failed to provide adequate instruction to students of Chinese ancestry who did not speak English, public school systems across the nation were expected to provide sufficient assistance to non-English-speaking students to enable them to succeed in school.

Perhaps the greatest impetus for new programs for students with special needs came the year after the *Lau* decision, when Congress passed Public Law 94-142, the Education of the Handicapped Act. In 1975, the year PL 94-142 was adopted, FCPS provided service to 1,875 special education students. A decade later, during a period when overall school enrollments were declining, the special education population had risen to 5,292. If the scope of FCPS's education empire was expanding, much of the credit belonged to the federal government.

A Commitment to Innovation

Just because a school system is large and blessed with abundant resources does not mean that it is necessarily innovative. During the '60s, however, the actions of Fairfax policymakers and educational leaders demonstrated that they wanted their school system not only to be high-performing and well-organized, but innovative as well. A special report released by Superintendent Funderburk in September of 1966 proudly cited 30 innovative programs that recently had been implemented (Proposal for the Operation of a Center for Effecting Educational Change, January 12, 1967). Among the listed programs were the following:

Academic subjects taught in foreign language
Adult basic education
Automatic data processing

Dining room hostesses
East Asian civilization
History of Russia
IBM student scheduling
Language experience approach in reading
Latin American civilization

New intermediate building concept
New physical science program
Nongraded programs
Pilot math program
Replacement teacher pool
School services division
School-within-a-school
String music program
Three new home economics courses

So heavily invested in educational change and improvement had Fairfax become, in fact, that the Superintendent felt compelled to apply for a Title III grant to better coordinate new initiatives. As noted earlier, his effort was rewarded with funding to create the Center for Effecting Educational Change in 1967.

Between 1962 and 1972, FCPS experimented with ungraded primary programs, programmed teaching materials, individualized instruction, open education, open-space design schools, and classrooms organized around learning centers (Kheradmand, 2002). When Dr. S. John Davis became Superintendent in September of 1970, he promoted team teaching, a thematic approach to teaching high school English, heterogeneous grouping for instruction, and curriculum-based district tests (Program of Studies tests).

Innovation was not limited to instructional practice, student grouping, and curriculum content. As Fairfax grew and new programs proliferated, the need for improved ways of organizing the school system became apparent. Before W. T. Woodson stepped down as Superintendent in 1961, he pointed out the "need for a study of the organization and operation of the Fairfax County School System exclusive of curriculum and instruction" (Hinkle, 1971, p. 191). When management consultants were commissioned to prepare a report in 1964 on the school system's efforts to keep pace with school construction needs, they also recommended that serious consideration be given to district reorganization:

> Seven persons report directly to the superintendent. The recommended planning unit could be an eighth. This appears to be an unreasonable span of control, and therefore the total organization of the schools should be carefully considered in the near future. ("School Plant Planning and Organization Audit," 1964, p. 34)

A year later Superintendent Funderburk, in his annual report, added his voice to calls for district reorganization: "In the next few years, a means to decentralize our large and sprawling school division must be found, to the extent that outside professional consultation may be necessary to accomplish this." (Superintendent's Annual Report, 1964-65)

Fairfax County Public Schools added 7,500 students in the 1963-1964 school year, a growth rate of 8.5 percent. The operating budget jumped from $33.1 million to $39.2 million, with $4.3 million required simply to accommodate enrollment growth. Besides growing numbers of students, Fairfax was adding new programs and services. In 1965 Head Start centers were created, and the School-Community Relations Division was established, in part to handle the transition from a dual to a unitary school system. In 1966 the Adult Education Program was initiated. Two years later, half-day kindergartens were launched. The expansion of special programs and services contributed to organizational complexity and increased the possibility of communication and coordination problems.

During the mid-'60s, FCPS attempted to handle complexity by adding supervisory personnel and new organizational units. Figure 1.1 presents the organization chart for Fairfax County Public Schools in 1963. In 1964 the Department of Instruction sought to "provide better coordination between schools and central office" by adding new supervisors of social studies and industrial arts, a new helping teacher in mathematics, and a full-time coordinator of adult education and summer school, as well as upgrading a supervisor of vocational education to a director. The following school year was marked by the creation of a Department of Construction and a Department of School Services, which coordinated custodial duties, distribution, warehousing, maintenance, plant operations, and food services (Berry, Chamberlin, and Goodloe, 2001). Supervision of instruction also was enhanced that year by the addition of 10 assistant principals, whose primary responsibility was to work directly with teachers on instructional improvement. These stop-gap measures, however, were no substitute for the fundamental reorganization called for by Superintendents Woodson and Funderburk.

The first step toward reorganization took place in 1967, when the School Board endorsed a plan drafted by Funderburk that by 1970 would divide the school system into five separate operational areas, each with an Area Superintendent responsible for supervising the schools in his area. Funderburk was careful to distinguish his decentralization plan from those that had created considerable controversy in large cities like New York (Funderburk, 1969; Jacoby 1968). While the latter were prompted by demands from minority groups for greater community control, the Fairfax plan constituted, at least in the Superintendent's thinking, an "internal administrative reorganization" intended to improve the efficiency of key supervisory personnel and narrow the distance between the schools and top-level leadership.

In 1967 the School Board retained the services of Cresap, McCormick & Paget to conduct a management audit of the school system's organization and operations. By the time the audit was completed in early 1968, Funderburk had appointed his first two Area Superintendents, and he was preparing to select a third. The consultant's report found that school board members were "too involved in detailed operating problems and as a result there are major gaps in Board policies and long-range planning" ("Decentralize School Setup, Fairfax Told," *The Washington Post*,

Figure 1.1
Organization Chart of Fairfax County Public Schools—1963

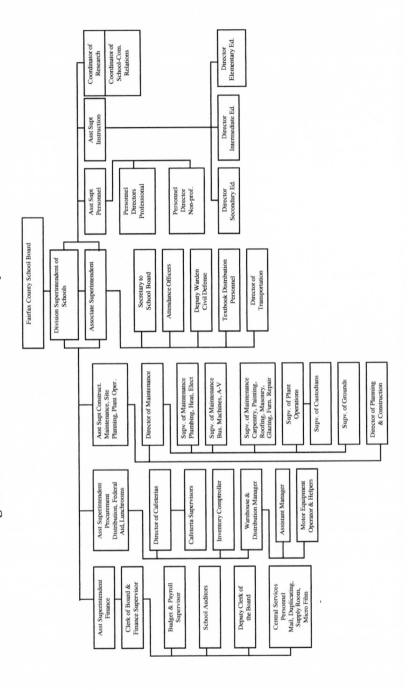

February 15, 1968). Among the other conclusions drawn in the final report were the following:

> The present organization...is cumbersome and unwieldy. The central office staff has not given adequate attention to broad policy and long-range planning problems.There is an overlapping of functions among the Assistant Superintendents.

> The central office staff, including the majority of the instructional assistance resources, has tended to concentrate on headquarters duties; consequently field efforts have been reduced. There is a lack of coordination among central office staff activities. (Cresap, McCormick & Paget, 1967)

The consultant's report went on to make a variety of recommendations, including the establishment of only three Area Administrative Offices, rather than the five called for in Funderburk's plan. Five Area Administrative Offices, each with an Area Superintendent and staff, would be inefficient and produce coordination problems, according to the consultant. The report also called for the creation of an Assistant for Planning, who would report to the Division Superintendent, and Citizens' Advisory Committees appointed by the School Board to advise the Division and Area Superintendents. Instructional and support personnel would be assigned to Area offices, thereby placing them in closer organizational proximity to schools. The central office, meanwhile, would concentrate on systemwide planning, analysis, coordination, and control.

The FCPS School Board supported the consultant's decentralization plan, eventually deciding to create four Area Administrative Offices, each headed by an Area Superintendent. Funderburk expressed reservations with the revised decentralization plan and what he regarded as the erosion of central office leadership (Berry, Chamberlin, and Goodloe, 2001). While supportive of placing "front line" personnel in the field, where they could be more responsive to school-based educators and the community, he preferred his version of "centralized decentralization" to the divided leadership threatened by the creation of the four semiautonomous Area Superintendents called for in the School Board's plan. Each Area Superintendent would be responsible for more schools, school personnel, and students than most Division Superintendents in Virginia. Displeasure with School Board support for the new decentralization arrangement was cited as the primary reason for Funderburk's retirement in 1969 (Berry, Chamberlin, and Goodloe, 2001).

The Area Administrative Offices with their Area Superintendents remained the basic organizational structure of Fairfax County Public Schools until the turn of the century. Reflecting back on his lengthy tenure with Fairfax County Public Schools, Deputy Superintendent Alan Leis identified the division of the school system into four areas as one of the pivotal events in the district's history. Decentralization enabled supervisory personnel to maintain close and effective contact with school-based personnel despite rapid growth. In Leis's words, "The school system was just growing too rapidly to meet the needs of schools from Mt. Vernon to Great Falls. There was a real feeling that central administration was getting too detached from most schools." As the decade of the '70s unfolded, however, it became clear that coping with enrollment growth would not continue to be the central challenge facing county educators. Instead, the new decade brought with it slowing growth and eventual enrollment decline, budget problems, and growing concerns about student performance.

Sinking into the '70s

As the Vietnam War wound down and the scandals of the Nixon presidency heated up, the mood of America lost much of the exuberance that had characterized the '60s. Where once possibilities ruled, problems prevailed. The economy began to sputter, the victim of deficit spending to sustain the war, a plethora of costly new social programs, and overdependence on foreign oil. Though still well-off compared to many localities, Fairfax County and its schools did not escape hard times.

The rapid growth rate of school enrollments slowed considerably in the early '70s. Had all parts of the county shared equally in the slowed growth, the school system could have begun to reduce its capital improvement and building initiatives. Unfortunately, the western part of the county continued to grow at a rate rivaling the '60s, while the eastern part of the county lost school-age population. As a consequence, new schools still were needed, despite an overall stabilizing of FCPS enrollments and an economic downturn. Overcrowding became a substantial enough concern that school officials considered switching eight schools to year-round schedules (Landres, 1973). Voter approval of bonds for building new schools and adding to existing schools, once considered virtually automatic in Fairfax, no longer could be counted on. A $60 million school bond referendum in November of 1974 was soundly defeated (Sims, 1974). Even tougher times lay ahead.

At the same time that education funds were becoming less plentiful, student achievement started to decline. Scores on the Scholastic Aptitude Tests began to fall. Educators were accused of grade inflation and neglect of the "basics." While Fairfax County students still out-performed their counterparts in other Virginia school systems, they slipped in the early '70s when compared to national norms (Division of Research and Testing, Information Memo #2, 1973). *Commitment to Education*, a Fairfax County Public Schools report published in 1973, reported that the number of students reading below grade level was rising. Some Fairfax intermediate schools reported between 30 and 40 percent of eighth graders were reading below grade level. A 1974 opinion poll of Fairfax County parents found that 73 percent believed the top priority for the school year should be finding improved ways to teach reading (Kheradmand, 2002).

Declining student achievement and a tightening economy caused many people to question rising education expenditures and demand more responsible action on the part of educators. *Accountability* became the new watchword for politicians, policymakers, and pundits. The term had been introduced into the public debate over education by President Richard Nixon:

> In his March 3rd (1970) Education Message, President Nixon stated, "From these considerations we derive another new concept: *Accountability*. School administrators and school teachers alike are responsible for their performance, and it is in their interest as well as in the interest of their pupils that they be held accountable." (Lessinger, 1971, pp. 62–63)

Soon after Nixon's remarks, states began enacting policies designed to increase educational accountability. Virginia was no exception. Drawing on a 1968 amendment to the state constitution that mandated "high quality" public schools, the Virginia Board of Education ordered Standards of Quality (SOQ) to be developed

(Duke and Reck, 2003). Modeled after business benchmarks, the SOQ provided guidelines regarding education personnel, materials, programs, and management. School systems were required to develop planning and management objectives aimed at bringing them into line with the SOQ. Enacted by the General Assembly in August of 1971 and implemented on July 1, 1972, the SOQ foreshadowed the increasing role of the state in local education.

Responding to the need for greater quality control over what was taught, FCPS developed grade-level objectives for the basic academic subjects in 1971 (Lecos, 1980, p. 6). These objectives constituted the basis for the school system's Program of Studies, which served as the foundation for all instructional policy in Fairfax County. In 1974 assessment experts from the county's Division of Research and Testing, in collaboration with curriculum specialists from the Department of Instructional Services, developed county tests aligned with the Program of Studies. This ambitious initiative predated by more than two decades the state of Virginia's effort to promote educational accountability through the use of standards-based testing. It would not be the last time Fairfax County found itself ahead of the curve.

When W. T. Woodson retired in 1961, he could feel confident that his school district was making good progress on the highway to educational excellence. By the time S. John Davis took over the superintendency in 1970, it had become apparent that there would be detours along the way.[4] In one area, however, Fairfax County Public Schools would be spared the disruptions that confronted many other school systems in the new decade. As a result of having desegregated relatively early, FCPS did not have to deal with court-ordered busing, as did Richmond and many other large school systems, nor did it have to face the virulent white backlash that marked the desegregation of Boston's schools.

The ability of Fairfax to desegregate its schools relatively early and with little turmoil may have been due as much to the small size of the black population as to enlightened local attitudes. In 1971 about 3 percent or 4,000 of the county's 136,000 students were black. The percentage of black students had dropped substantially since 1954. The reason why the number of black students was low probably had a lot to do with restrictive housing policies. Robert E. Frye, the third African-American school board member in Fairfax County and the first to be elected, remembered the difficulties faced by blacks trying to move to Fairfax County in the '60s and '70s. Shortly after he and his family moved to Reston, a planned community and one of the first areas in Fairfax to advertise an open housing policy, the original developer was forced to go out of business. The new developer, under pressure from lending institutions, abandoned ads picturing blacks and whites living together in Reston.

Aware that race had not disappeared as a social issue with the cessation of segregated schools, the Fairfax County School Board unanimously adopted a human relations policy in the fall of 1971 (Whitaker, 1971). The policy pledged to fight all vestiges of racism and guarantee equal rights for students and employees. Further, the School Board committed to helping students and staff members understand and value all minority groups. It is worth noting, however, that prior to the School Board's vote, several board members "expressed doubt that the board has the authority to enforce all the 'guarantees' outlined in the policy statement" (Whitaker, 1971).

Less than a year later, representatives of Fairfax's black community, led by Mona Blake, the School Board's first black member, were back before the board calling for "immediate improvement" in matters related to race (Landres, 1972). Among their proposals were sensitivity training for school personnel, a course in black history that would serve as an alternative to the required course in Virginia history, and attention to the high expulsion rate for black students. In the years to come the voices of black residents would be joined by growing numbers of immigrants to form a chorus calling for a more equal distribution of educational benefits.

CHAPTER 2

A Ten-Year Trial

For a large suburban school system like Fairfax, no year passes without its share of challenges. Between 1976 and 1985, however, Fairfax County Public Schools, along with school systems across the nation, faced a series of extraordinarily difficult circumstances, including enrollment decline, a stalled economy, and mounting pressures to address students with special needs. As if these problems were not daunting enough, Fairfax struggled to find the right leader to guide it through troubled waters. The mark of a great school system, however, is not only how it handles expansion, ample resources, and generally favorable conditions, but also how it weathers periods of retrenchment, turmoil, and uncertainty. That Fairfax emerged from its 10-year trial with a fine reputation largely intact and poised to press forward toward even greater accomplishments was a credit to the school system and its community.

The chapter begins by examining enrollment decline and its consequences for FCPS. This discussion is followed by a review of the economic problems that plagued the school system during the late '70s and early "80s and its search for stable leadership. Two reasons why Fairfax escaped this period with relatively little damage was its steadfast commitment to respond constructively to students with special needs and its persistent openness to new and innovative ways of doing things. These aspects of district operations are addressed at the end of the chapter.

The End of the Baby Boom

Something very unusual happened when the doors of Fairfax schools opened in September of 1976. Fewer students entered the schools than the previous year. For the next eight years, enroll-

41

KEY DATES FOR FAIRFAX COUNTY PUBLIC SCHOOLS:
1976-1985

1976 School enrollment for FCPS drops

Division of Research and Testing is created

1977 Virginia Supreme Court disallows collective bargaining by public employees

1978 School Board adopts policies governing school closings

1979 L. Linton Deck appointed Superintendent

1980 Superintendent Deck reorganizes central office

1981 FCPS receives federal approval for its ESL program

1982 William J. Burkholder appointed Superintendent

1983 School Board agrees to study the achievement gap between white and African-American students

1984 Merit pay plan is presented to School Board

FCPS adopts a long-range plan to improve minority achievement

Superintendent Burkholder resigns in dispute over his compensation package

1985 Robert R. Spillane appointed Superintendent

Thomas Jefferson High School for Science and Technology opens

---

ments continued to drop. America's—and Fairfax's—experiment with population explosion had come to an end, at least temporarily. According to state statistics, FCPS enrollment peaked at 145,385 students in 1974-1975. The following year saw a slight decrease to 145,300 students. By 1982-1983, enrollment had settled at 122,646, more than 22,000 fewer students than 1974-1975. Fairfax would go on to complete the century and enter the new millennium with steadily increasing numbers of students. By 2004 enrollments exceeded 166,000 students, making Fairfax the nation's 12th largest school system.

Someone unfamiliar with the impact of declining enrollments in school systems might assume that the primary consequence would be school closings. For Fairfax, the process of dealing with declining enrollments was hardly so straightforward and simple. First of all, trying to close a school, especially a high school, can generate considerable controversy. Community sentiments, like land mass around a coral reef, build up around neighborhood schools. Closing a school can adversely affect property values and even threaten the very existence of a neighborhood. Another problem concerns the fact that neighborhoods do not lose all their children at the same time. Numbers dwindle slowly as a rule, forcing school systems like Fairfax to consider redrawing school boundaries. This process ultimately can result in proposals to close certain schools, but not before one neighborhood is pitted against another neighborhood in a contest to see whose school will survive. To make the drama of declining enrollments even more difficult, parts of Fairfax County actually continued to grow, while other parts declined. Consequently, the school system was forced into the awkward position of proposing to build new schools in the western part of the county at the same time it sought to close schools in the eastern part of the county. Not only were adjacent neighborhoods placed at odds, but the county itself was divided between areas of growth and areas of decline. Maintaining a focus on educational quality under such circumstances can be extremely difficult.

Realizing the sensitive nature of official responses to declining enrollments, Fairfax County Public Schools tried to involve citizens as much as possible in the process of determining what to do. A citizens' task force in 1977 reported that 25 elementary schools enrolled fewer than 350 students (Locke, April 6, 1978). Elementary schools under 350 students typically had too few students to fill two classes per grade, thereby making them relatively expensive to operate. By 1982 the number of underenrolled facilities was projected to be 60 elementary schools. Between 1974 and 1978, Fairfax closed five schools, and all but one of these closings was greeted by angry protests from parents. In an effort to minimize controversy and rancor, the School Board in the late '70s sought to develop a comprehensive policy to guide the closing of schools. One proposal targeted schools for closing when their cost per student had risen significantly higher than the countywide average for three consecutive years. Another proposal made schools scheduled for major renovations eligible for closing. The school closing policy finally adopted by the School Board on November 2, 1978, included both of these criteria along with additional guidelines. When an elementary school was selected for a closing study, adjacent schools also had to be studied. According to the policy, a community advisory committee of representatives from affected schools would participate in conducting the closing study, which needed to include considerations of natural boundaries, safety hazards, and transportation barriers.

A year after adopting the policy, 29 elementary schools were identified for possible closing (Dougherty, December 1, 1979). The School Board braced itself for parent protests and organized resistance. After a year of input from affected neighborhoods, newly appointed Superintendent L. Linton Deck proposed closing eight elementary schools in the eastern part of the county. Community leaders registered shock in light of the fact that citizen advisory committees had recommended closing only three schools (Dougherty, April 24, 1980). In the face of intense lobbying, several board members indicated that they were unlikely to support the new Superintendent's recommendation. This would not be the only occasion on which Fairfax's new leader and its School Board failed to see eye to eye.

If there was a lesson learned regarding Fairfax's new school closing policy, it was not to expect gratitude from community members just because they were granted an opportunity to participate in the process of studying which schools should be closed. Parents and their allies, who rallied support for the seven elementary schools that eventually were closed during the first application of the new policy, were just as bitter and critical of the school system as if they had never participated in deliberations at all. Advocates for one of the seven schools even went so far as to take the school system to court, but the judge sided with the School Board (Dougherty, July 24, 1980).

If proposing to shut down elementary schools causes community sentiments to flare up, trying to close a secondary school can produce a full-scale conflagration. It was only a matter of time before the declining elementary enrollments of the late '70s caught up with Fairfax's intermediate and high schools. Faced with the prospect of closing secondary schools, educators are fond of extolling the benefits of smaller schools. Allowing some schools to be downsized, in fact, was one of six options for coping with lower secondary enrollments that were presented to the School Board in the winter of 1981 by Superintendent Deck (Gordon, February 13, 1981). Other possible courses of action included closing some secondary schools, making boundary changes to balance enrollments across schools, adding teachers to smaller schools to maintain levels of course offerings, reducing the variety of course offerings while maintaining the same number of teachers, and combining several options. In early spring, however, the School Board decided to take no immediate action, but to spend several years studying the situation (Hodge, April 2, 1981).

The hoped-for calm was broken in the fall of 1981, when the School Board, under pressure from the rapidly growing western part of the county, proposed a $57.2 million bond issue to build five new schools and four other facilities as well as renovate nine schools. Many people questioned why the school system would consider such a project, when schools in the eastern part of the county were begging for students. Board members tried to remind critics that two decades earlier residents of the western part of the county had supported school construction in the then burgeoning eastern half of the county. Parents living in the west also made it known that they opposed busing their children over the county's heavily trafficked roads in order for them to attend schools in the east.

The western part of the county eventually prevailed, while eastern residents waited anxiously to see if the School Board would recommend closing any of their secondary schools. In January of 1984, the School Board adopted a new policy governing secondary school boundary changes (Latimer, January 27, 1984). High schools should have at least 1,400 students, but should not exceed 90 percent of their enrollment capacity "in order to ensure that their educational programs are effective." The School Board agreed to a provision that it would not consider studying a secondary school for possible closure unless enrollment dropped below 1,250 for a high school and 625 for an intermediate school. Boundary lines might be redrawn if a school exceeded 90 percent of its capacity. The School Board also issued guidelines indicating that new intermediate schools should be built to accommodate 1,000 students and new high schools 2,000 students. Their action put to rest for the moment any prospect of a district commitment to smaller, more "personalized" secondary schools.

To implement the new policy, an enormous amount of planning and demographic study was required. Much of this work was undertaken by Fairfax's Facilities Planning Office and its nine-member staff. Operating out of an obscure office dubbed "the War Room," planners studied maps, charts, and computer printouts in order to provide guidance regarding school closings and boundary changes. While the Facilities Planning staff handled details, actual proposals for changes derived from a group of top-level leaders, including the Superintendent, the Assistant Superintendent for Facility Services, the four Area Superintendents, and various community leaders. The School Board was the last stop on the line, and its vote was required before a school closing or boundary change became official. It is important to note that, until 1995, school board members in Fairfax, and indeed throughout Virginia, were appointed, not elected. Appointments in Fairfax were made by members of the county's Board of Supervisors, the members of which were popularly elected. The supervisors controlled the pursestrings of the school district, since Virginia did not permit school systems to exercise independent taxing authority.

The moment parents in the eastern part of the county dreaded came close on the heels of adoption of the School Board's new school closing policy. On February 9, 1984, Superintendent William J. Burkholder, who had replaced Linton Deck in June of 1982, called for the closing of two intermediate schools in the east. Having learned their lesson previously, school officials maintained secrecy regarding which schools would be studied for closing until the School Board met. Even School Board members were not given advance copies of the proposal. Despite these precautionary measures, 800 people packed Fairfax High School to learn about which schools made the "hit list."

In late March the School Board decided to close one of the two intermediate schools—Whittier in Falls Church—and delay consideration of the second intermediate school. At the same meeting, attendance boundaries were changed for 50 schools. Board members, reflecting the preferences of their constituents, haggled over virtually every proposal (Latimer, April 27, 1984). Coping with enrollment declines and boundary shifts was placing a heavy strain on relationships among Board members. Circumstances would deteriorate even more before enrollments finally began to rise sufficiently to ease the pressure to close schools.

Perhaps the bitterest battle over school closing involved two eastern high schools—Groveton and Ft. Hunt. Before the smoke finally cleared, advocates for each school had formed groups dedicated to preventing closing, former friends stopped speaking to each other, charges of racism and elitism were hurled at defenders of Ft. Hunt, and Board members squared off against each other (Carton, March 14, 1985). Parents fighting to keep Ft. Hunt a high school raised almost $15,000, took out full-page newspaper ads to promote their cause, organized a massive letter-writing campaign, and even produced a booklet recounting their school's history and accomplishments. Public hearings resulted in heated interchanges and accusations. Lack of parent and community interest in school business was not a problem about which Fairfax school officials had to worry. In recognition of the importance of community relations to the school system, Superintendent Burkholder, in fact, created a Department of Community Relations headed by a new Assistant Superintendent.

The era of school closing unofficially ended with the announcement on March 14, 1985, that Ft. Hunt High School—the school derided by Groveton advocates as the "country club on the Potomac"—would be converted to an intermediate school. The final vote—6 to 4—reflected the deep division among Board members. By the fall of 1985, Fairfax's school-age population again was on the rise, signaling a shift in focus for district planners and the commencement of a new period of expansion.

Where Did All the Money Go?

When Fairfax school officials unveiled the school system's proposed budget for 1977-1978, it came with the admonition that funding reductions could adversely affect academic programs (Murphy, January 6, 1977). To construct the $239 million budget, FCPS initiated a modified form of "zero-based budgeting." Instead of beginning the budget-building process with each program's budget for the previous year and deciding whether or not cuts needed to be made, "zero-based budgeting" required officials to start from scratch and provide new justifications for every program and budget line. During this time of tight money, Fairfax County Public Schools also expanded the budgetary authority of school principals. The shift to more "site-based budgeting" marked the beginning of a quarter century's efforts to increase the huge school system's responsiveness to the needs of individual schools.

The proposed budget for 1977-1978 included a $4.4 million cut based on economizing efforts and projected enrollment losses amounting to more than 2,000 students (156 fewer teaching positions). Ineffective programs were axed along with programs for which federal aid had been terminated, replacement of school buses was curtailed, and six positions in adult education were eliminated. These savings were offset, however, by a proposed 5.4 percent salary increase for most school employees, higher fuel and utility bills, capital improvements for older schools, additional spending on special education to meet state requirements, and the initiation of English-as-a-Second-Language programs. Superintendent Davis warned that, in light of shrinking federal and state aid, local taxpayers would have to pick up a larger percentage of the tab. Instead of 58 percent of the school budget, county residents would have to cover 62 percent of the new budget. Davis also cautioned that, if the proposed budget was rejected, he had no alternative but to renegotiate salary increases for employees. With 87 percent of Fairfax's budget devoted to salaries and benefits, there simply was no other way to effect reductions.

The issues that arose in preparing Fairfax's 1977-1978 school budget would become persistent themes over the ensuing decades. The school system no longer could count on increasing allocations from Washington, D.C., and Richmond, despite the fact that the flow of government directives rarely slowed. Unfunded and underfunded mandates, in fact, would increasingly become a point of tension between Fairfax County Public Schools and government officials.

A month after introducing the 1977–1978 budget, Fairfax leaders anticipated the need for more cuts. Efforts were made to lobby Richmond for greater latitude in meeting state class size guidelines (Locke, February 3, 1977). The General Assembly's mandated class size cap of 28 students in grades one through three was estimated to represent an additional budgetary commitment of between $1.7 and $2.4 million. Without more money from the state, a large school system like FCPS would be hard-pressed to meet the new requirement.

Besides new mandates, another issue that refused to go away involved employee salaries. Great school systems depend on great teachers and administrators. Attracting and keeping talented personnel in a region where the cost of living was relatively high required competitive salaries. Inflation during the '70s ate away at modest salary increases and led to growing morale problems and mounting pressure from teachers for substantial improvements in wages and benefits. With declining revenue, school officials were forced to consider various trade-offs in order to respond to teacher demands. School system leaders were challenged to ensure that trade-offs such as higher class sizes did not adversely impact student learning and academic quality.

In its efforts to protect salary increases for teachers and administrators, the School Board sometimes encountered resistance from the Board of Supervisors. While the supervisors determined the amount of local revenue available to the school district, school board members controlled which specific items in the budget would be increased, decreased, or eliminated. During periods of retrenchment, the Board of Supervisors tried to influence these decisions, typically opposing pay increases for teachers and ambitious capital improvement programs (Locke, September 21, 1978). School Board members countered by insisting that salary improvements were crucial to maintaining a first-class faculty and threatening to cut popular programs and postpone efforts to meet state accreditation standards.

The early '80s found school system officials annually battling for resources with the Board of Supervisors and, when their efforts fell short of the mark, trying to defend various budget cuts and postponed improvements. Special education attracted attention in the spring of 1980, when parents and teachers alleged that inadequate funding had resulted in delays of up to a full school year in placing eligible students in special education programs (Bauer, May 23, 1980). The next year a reduction in federal aid forced reductions in remedial reading and increased prices for school lunches (Walsh, July 10, 1981). Vocational education took a hit in 1982, when the School Board decided to eliminate a third of the school system's vocational education classes (Moore, February 4, 1982).

Table 2.1 presents the numbers of teachers and students in FCPS for each school year from 1974-1975 through 1984-1985. The school system's success in maintaining professional staff numbers despite difficult economic times and declining enrollments is apparent. While the number of students declined annually until 1983-1984, the size of the teaching force increased every year except 1976-1977 and 1982-1983.

Table 2.2 indicates the numbers of personnel in a variety of categories from 1973-1974 through 1984-1985. Despite the challenges of a decade's retrenchment, the ranks of Fairfax's central office administrators and support personnel, for the most part, continued to grow. Many of the new positions were associated with new programs mandated by law and required to address the needs of special populations of students. In 1984-85, the first year in which such data were reported, FCPS employed 1,044 instructional aides. A substantial number of these assistants were involved in special education and compensatory programs.

One reason that Fairfax County Public Schools weathered the economic problems of the '70s and early '80s without decimating its ranks was the strength of local property values. The true value of locally taxed property, for example, rose from a little less than

Table 2.1
Numbers of Teachers and Students in
Fairfax County Public Schools: 1974–75 to 1984–85[1]

School Year	Teachers	Students
1974-75	6,869	145,385
1975-76	7,202	145,300
1976-77	7,096	143,720
1977-78	7,131	140,702
1978-79	7,177	138,588
1979-80	7,181	128,653[2]
1980-81	7,323	126,829
1981-82	7,361	124,490
1982-83	7,298	122,646
1983-84	7,306	122,823
1984-85	7,484	123,827

1. Statistics were taken from the Annual Reports of the Superintendent of Public Instruction of the Commonwealth of Virginia.
2. In 1979-80, the state switched from total enrollment figures to average daily membership (ADM) figures for school divisions.

$5 billion in 1973-74 to over $13 billion in 1978–79. This meant that the wealth per child in Fairfax County climbed from $38,309 to $102,083 over a six-year period. FCPS ranked second only to Arlington, Virginia, in annual per pupil expenditures, with a figure of $1,460 in 1978-79.

Tough times revealed the School Board's willingness to engage in aggressive politicking. When the Reagan administration threatened to cut federal impact aid, the School Board countered by recommending that the 2,000 students attending public school at Fort Belvoir be charged tuition. When the Justice Department squelched this ploy, the School Board sought to have Fort Belvoir declared a separate school district (Moore, November 19, 1981). When the governor threatened to cut state aid, the School Board stepped up its lobbying efforts in Richmond and declared its inability to respond appropriately to state mandates if education funds were reduced. When the Board of Supervisors pressed the School Board to reduce its budget, the School Board refused to allow supervisors to influence where cuts would be made. Furthermore, School Board members made sure that the cuts they endorsed would place the Board of Supervisors in an awkward position vis-à-vis the public. By the time enrollments began to climb again and the economy perked up, the School Board could take pride in its efforts to prevent serious damage to the school system's core programs and talented staff.

Table 2.2

Assorted Staffing Figures for Fairfax County Public Schools: 1973–74 to 1984–85[3]

School Year	Assistant Superintendents	Other Central Office Adm's	Secretaries/ Clerical	Health Service	Pupil Transportation	Plant Operation and Maintenance
1973-74	7	82	814	36	661	1,689
1974-75	10	131.9	776	39	680	1,690
1975-76	10	170	886	45	684	1,703
1976-77	10	101	888	0	732	1,687
1977-78	10	122	884	0	768	1,697
1978-79	10	140	819	0	751	1,719
1979-80	10	136	835	0	781	1,729
1980-81	15	140	892	0	802	1,781
1981-82	15	196	853	0	802	1,786
1982-83	13	179	858	0	805	1,782
1983-84	13	184	829	108	806	1,795
1984-85	14	211	872	110	893	1,814

3. Statistics were taken from the *Annual Reports of the Superintendent of Public Instruction of the Commonwealth of Virginia*.

The Quest for Stable Leadership

It is the rare leader who can sail unbuffeted through stormy times. Superintendent S. John (Jack) Davis managed to do so from 1970, when he moved from his position as Area Superintendent to Division Superintendent, until the spring of 1979. Of his tenure during this period, *The Washington Post* (Knight, May 17, 1979) reported:

> For nine years, Fairfax County School Superintendent S. John Davis successfully managed a delicate balancing act. He presided over painful decisions about school closings, principal transfers, and a redrawing of school boundaries, yet he maintained the respect of the people most affected.

In late April of 1979, however, Fairfax teachers, along with colleagues in two other Northern Virginia school systems, voted no confidence in their Superintendent. Two-thirds of Fairfax's 7,000 teachers agreed that Davis had not done enough to dissuade the Board of Supervisors from rejecting a 9.4 percent pay raise that they demanded. Targeting the Superintendent represented a marked shift in strategy for the teachers, a shift occasioned by the Virginia Supreme Court's 1977 declaration that negotiated contracts between professional organizations and local governing bodies were illegal (Murphy, February 17, 1977). In the wake of the ruling, 18 Virginia school systems, including Fairfax County, no longer were permitted to collectively bargain with teachers. Unable to express their concerns directly to the School Board at the bargaining table, the Fairfax Teachers' Association opted to focus on the Superintendent. The Superintendent was responsible for preparing and defending the school system's budget. If teachers' demands for salary improvement went unheeded, the Superintendent must bear the burden of responsibility. To amplify their dissatisfaction, many teachers implemented a "work-to-rule" job action in which they refused to undertake extracurricular duties.

In reality, of course, the legal responsibility for the school system's budget rested with the School Board and the Board of Supervisors. Davis, however, served as the fall guy for teachers frustrated over their loss of the right to bargain. By the time the Fairfax Teachers' Association took its no confidence vote, Davis had become one of the leading candidates for Virginia's Superintendent of Public Instruction. Whether the simmering discontent among teachers had prompted Davis to seek the position is unknown, but associates noted that he was deeply hurt by the no confidence vote. On May 18, 1979, he resigned the Fairfax superintendency to accept the state's top education post.

On May 24, 1979, the School Board named Associate Superintendent William Burkholder as interim Superintendent, while a national search was conducted for Davis's successor. It would not be the last time that the veteran Fairfax educator would be called on to step into the breach left by a departing leader. During Burkholder's first stint, Fairfax County Public Schools became the largest school system in the Washington metropolitan region, surpassing Maryland's Prince George's County Public Schools. FCPS actually had not grown in student numbers; rather it lost fewer students than Prince George's.

Fairfax's six-month search for a new leader came to an end on November 19, 1979, with the announcement by the School Board that L. Linton Deck, head of the Orange County, Florida, schools, had been chosen to be the new Superintendent. In his first press conference, Deck acknowledged that Fairfax faced a serious teacher morale problem (Dougherty, November 20, 1979). He promised to study teachers' concerns, but in an interview just 10 days after his appointment, Deck made it clear that he did not feel salaries were the only source of teacher discontent (Dougherty, November 29, 1979).

Judging by his first moves as Superintendent of FCPS, boosting teacher morale was not Deck's only concern. Soon after taking over, he proposed a series of reorganization moves that included reassigning existing administrative personnel and realigning several central office departments (Dougherty, June 5, 1980). A new position, Assistant Superintendent for Vocational and Adult Education, was created, along with three new units—the Management Services Department, the Resources Development Office, and the Program Development Office. One consequence of the restructuring was that only three administrators would report directly to Deck—Deputy Superintendents Jacqueline Benson and William Burkholder and Financial Services Associate Superintendent Myron Cale. A spokesman for Fairfax teachers expressed his fear that the new arrangement could result in Deck being cut off from the flow of information from the front lines (Dougherty, June 12, 1980). He went on to contrast Burkholder's accessibility to teachers during his brief term as interim Superintendent with Deck's perceived aloofness.

Also during his first year on the job, Deck announced that every administrator in the school system, including himself, would be required to work as a substitute teacher for at least one day in the 1980-81 school year ("Back to Class in Fairfax," September 11, 1980). The bold move was designed to keep administrators "keenly aware of life in the classroom."

Despite the reservations of many teachers and some school administrators, Deck's future at the helm in Fairfax looked rosy in January of 1981, when he accepted a pay raise and four-year contract from the School Board. A mere 18 months later, however, newspapers announced that Deck had been forced to resign his position (Moore, June 26, 1982). No single incident appeared to have led to the School Board's action. Rather, an accumulating number of grievances, ranging from poor relations with community and political leaders to failure to rein in the school system's mushrooming budget, finally passed the tipping point. Critics also cited Deck's "abrasive, overbearing personality" and "you follow or get the hell out of my way" leadership as contributing factors (Moore, June 26, 1982). At the time of his resignation, Deck was acknowledged to have been instrumental in pushing Fairfax into the Computer Age and fighting for more funding for new programs, but these were insufficient to offset complaints from virtually every stakeholder group. The specific reasons why various groups were upset with Deck ranged from the mundane—mishandling of school closings on a snowy day—to the meaningful—unpopular transfers of principals and a heavy-handed investigation of recruiting violations by members of the Mount Vernon High School athletic staff.

Probably the most appropriate comment on Deck's brief tenure is that his leadership style was not a good match for Fairfax County. Some leaders fit their surroundings, and others don't. Deck's confrontational nature and unwillingness to compromise, as much as his policies and positions, distanced him from key local leaders and stakeholder groups.

The man who succeeded Deck, first as acting Superintendent and then as the School Board's chosen replacement, was an excellent "fit" for Fairfax County. William J. Burkholder started out in 1956 as a Fairfax teacher and worked his way up the ladder to various central office posts, including interim Superintendent following S. John Davis's departure and Deputy Superintendent under Linton Deck. Burkholder's appointment was hailed by virtually every influential group, from community organizations to teachers and administrators. He was regarded as a person who cared about Fairfax County and who was willing to fight for school improvements and budget increases.

Burkholder's honeymoon, however, was destined to be brief. After less than 3 months as Superintendent, he upset the black community by eliminating one of two vacant positions as Deputy Superintendent. Burkholder claimed his move was intended to save money, but black leaders believed that he purposely passed over a popular black candidate who would have probably won the second vacant position if it had not been eliminated (Moore, September 29, 1982). Later that fall, Fairfax teachers picketed over modest proposed salary increases that failed to offset inflation. When Burkholder submitted his $449.5 million operating budget in January of 1983, a budget that he characterized as "austere," the only words of praise came from the Board of Supervisors (Zibart, January 5, 1983). A year later, Burkholder attempted to build a bigger salary increase into the budget, but teacher leaders expressed concern that it was paired with a proposal to introduce merit pay for teachers. Concerns also surfaced at the same time over disparities between the achievement of minority and white students in Fairfax County (Hodge, 1984).

Given the challenges he faced, few people were surprised when *The Washington Post* (Painton, June 14, 1984) reported that Burkholder planned to retire as of July 1, 1985. What did come as a surprise was the announcement several months later that the School Board had convinced Burkholder to stay on to complete "unfinished business" (Painton, September 7, 1984). One item on this agenda, according to Burkholder, involved narrowing the gap in achievement between minority and white students. Observers speculated that the School Board's efforts to find a replacement for Burkholder had failed to net a worthy candidate. Acceptable emperors for education empires apparently were in short supply.

Burkholder likely regretted his decision soon after he made it. The School Board, in order to woo him to postpone retirement, agreed to compensate Burkholder for a substantial amount of local and state retirement benefits that he would forfeit by remaining on the job. When Fairfax citizens learned that their Superintendent would receive $157,000 a year, more than twice the salary of Virginia's governor and the highest salary package for any Superintendent in the United States, the reaction was swift and highly critical. School Board members were told that Burkholder's salary would jeopardize their chances of gaining approval for an upcoming $74.8 million bond referendum (Painton, September 26, 1984). On September 27, 1984, Burkholder announced that he would quit his post because of the public outcry over his compensation. For the fourth time in five years, the School Board initiated a search for a new leader.

Expanding the Benefits of a Fairfax Education

Students of leadership are fond of linking organizational success to stable, high-quality leadership. To its credit, FCPS managed to press forward with efforts to address the needs of minority students and improve the overall performance of the school system's academic programs despite the game of musical chairs at the top. That Fairfax never lost sight of its educational mission during the turbulent years of the late '70s and early '80s can be traced to the commitment of key School Board members, the dedication of Fairfax's professional educators, the active involvement of the community, and the continuing concern for improvement that was becoming a hallmark of Fairfax's culture of educational excellence.

Total enrollment in Fairfax schools may have dwindled after 1975, but the percentage of minority and non-English-speaking students steadily rose. Between 1977 and 1985, for example, the percentage of minority students jumped from 9 to over 21 percent (Berry, et al., 2001). The demand for English as a Second Language and special education services also increased. Uncertain resources and pressure to retrench did not tempt Fairfax educators to scrimp on efforts to address their neediest students.

Symbolic and substantive efforts

On February 13, 1979, the U.S. Civil Rights Commission observed the 25th anniversary of the Brown decision by noting that nearly half of the nation's minority children still attended racially segregated schools ("Fairfax County Schools Found Succeeding in Integration Plan," 1979). The commission took the occasion to praise a few large-school systems, including Fairfax County, for making impressive progress toward "equality of education." Fairfax's success was attributed to a high percentage of white students, which presumably lessened the likelihood of large-scale white flight, and the absence of community groups "actively opposing desegregation." Fairfax's efforts to recruit and hire minority educators and provide systematic human relations training for all staff members drew particular praise from the commission report.

As reinforcing as were the report's comments about Fairfax County schools, Fairfax educators realized that they taught in an area where it was impossible to rest on their laurels. Four months after being lauded by the U.S. Civil Rights Commission, the county's Human Relations Advisory Committee presented a study that indicted the school system's suspension practices ("Black Pupils Suspended," 1979). The study found that 19 percent of black students had been suspended at least once as compared to 7 percent of white students. The chairman of the committee complained that the disturbing statistics had remained stable over time.

The pot continued to be stirred later that same year when the 25th anniversary of the Brown decision was marked by *The Washington Post*. The newspaper's education staff writer, Kerry Dougherty (December 6, 1979), compared suspension statistics for schools in Alexandria (46% black), Arlington (15.7% black), and Fairfax (5.75% black). While Alexandria and Arlington suspended 10.3 percent and 17.5 percent respectively, Fairfax topped the list by suspending one out of every five black students. The article went on to note substantial disparities between the reading and mathematics minimum competency test scores for black and white children. The achievement gap for reading in Fairfax was the lowest of the three school systems, but the 20.2 percent difference (97.5% pass rate for whites; 77.3% pass rate for blacks) was still much too large to ignore. The gap in mathematics achievement for Fairfax students was virtually the same as in reading (97.2% pass rate for whites; 77.3% pass rate for blacks). Arlington's gap was slightly lower than Fairfax's, while Alexandria's gap was a staggering 29.7 percent. Such depressing data prompted some black educators to claim that black students had been better off in segregated schools.

By 1984 Fairfax County had a different Superintendent and a somewhat rosier financial picture, but the achievement gap between black and white students persisted (Hodge, January 14, 1984). At the behest of Robert Frye, Fairfax's only black School Board member, a study of black and white achievement had been approved the previous year. The study was the only concession that Frye could wrestle from the School Board, when he failed to persuade his colleagues to designate the "improved performance of underachieving students" as a top priority for the school system.

The in-house study confirmed what many already knew—the achievement of black and Hispanic students lagged well behind that of their Asian and white peers (Fairfax County Public Schools, 1984). Black students also received a disproportionately large percentage of D's and F's, fewer slots in gifted programs (1.8%), and more recommendations for retention at grade level. Although black students made up only 10.3 percent of Fairfax kindergarten students in 1983, 24.1 percent of black kinder-garteners failed kindergarten. The dropout rate for black students—4.8 percent—was substantially greater than that for Hispanics (2.8%), Asians (2.3%), and whites (1.7%). When Frye heard about the results of the study, he found them "devastating because we have such a fine school system and black performance has been masked by the good overall performance" (Hodge, January 14, 1984, p. A-1).

Until 1984 Fairfax's efforts to facilitate integration had focused mainly on staff development, minority hiring, and symbolic gestures. An example of the last type of initiative was the School Board's decision to observe the birthday of Martin Luther King as a school holiday (Zibart, May 13, 1983). Robert Frye had worked for four years to secure board approval. When the decision finally was made to honor Dr. King in 1983, Fairfax County Public Schools became one of the first school systems in the nation to do so. Efforts to train Fairfax staff to work with black students, as noted in the preceding chapter, began soon after the desegregation of Fairfax schools. In the spring of 1978, FCPS again placed itself ahead of the curve, when it developed an ambitious minority hiring plan (Locke, March 30, 1978). The plan called for raising the number of minority teachers in five years to 10 percent of the total staff. When the plan was adopted in June, the percentage was increased to 11 percent to reflect the actual percentage of minority students attending Fairfax schools. The plan also included provisions to hire more women administrators.

Mounting concern over the persistent gap between the achievement of black and white students compelled Fairfax educators to look beyond affirmative action and symbolic gestures. The catalyst for action was the previously mentioned in-house report by the Advisory Committee on the Academic Performance of Minority Students in Fairfax County Public Schools (Fairfax County Public Schools, 1984). The report prompted school officials

in May of 1984 to unveil a long-range plan designed to close the
gap (Latimer, May 23, 1984). The plan was based on two central
principles. First, effectively addressing the needs of low-achieving
students required special funding outside of the regular operating
budget. Second, resources should be directed to particular schools
with high concentrations of minority students. These two principles would continue to guide school system efforts to help at-risk
students into the next century.

The 28-page plan contained a variety of provisions aimed at
raising minority achievement. In an effort to monitor the academic
needs of young children, second graders were to be tested. Target
schools were offered grants to develop interventions in reading,
mathematics, and interpersonal relations. Incentives were provided to attract outstanding teachers to work in schools with high
concentrations of minority and low-income students. The School
Board allocated $460,890 out of its $495.9 million 1984-1985
budget to initiate the new plan. Fairfax's financial commitment to
needy students would climb substantially over the coming years.

Addressing language and cultural diversity

As the number of non-English-speaking students in Fairfax
County grew, so too did the level of disagreement concerning how
best to educate them. The debate was not so much between groups
within Fairfax County as between FCPS and the federal government. When the U.S. Department of Education proposed a new
rule requiring local school systems receiving federal funds to institute bilingual education programs for non-English-speaking students, Esther Eisenhower, Director of Fairfax's English as a
Second Language (ESL) program protested (Dougherty, August 14,
1980). She pointed to data indicating that Fairfax's ESL students,
representing 56 language groups, scored exceptionally well on
standardized tests and were highly involved in extracurricular
activities. Eisenhower was quoted in *The Washington Post*
(Dougherty, August 14, 1980) as saying, "I challenge the federal
government, or anybody, to show me a program where children are
learning more than in Fairfax County."

Confidence in the effectiveness of Fairfax's ESL program led
the Board of Supervisors to threaten a legal challenge if the federal
government enacted the bilingual education requirement ("Fairfax
Board Will Challenge Rules on Bilingual Education," October 7,
1980). School officials noted that Fairfax's million-dollar-a-year

ESL program sped up the integration of the county's 2,700 non-English-speaking students into the educational mainstream.

Fairfax County Public Schools received a belated Christmas gift when the U.S. Department of Education announced at the beginning of 1981 that the county's ESL program fulfilled the civil rights standards for the new rule, even though it did not call for teaching foreign-born students in their native language ("Feds OK Fairfax ESL Plan," January 2, 1981). Fairfax County Public Schools had become a force to be reckoned with, not just in Richmond, but in the nation's capital as well. Government rules and regulations that were intended to correct deficiencies in the educational programs of underachieving school systems did not fit Fairfax County. It is worth noting that within a month of Fairfax's receipt of the federal letter of approval for its ESL program, newly appointed Secretary of Education Terrel Bell, representing the Reagan administration, withdrew the rule requiring bilingual education. President Reagan cited Fairfax's success with its ESL program as a prime reason why the federal government should leave educational decisions up to localities (Feinberg, March 4, 1981).

In the '80s, the ESL program developed by FCPS became a national model for the education of language minority students. Newly arriving non-English-speakers were evaluated and registered at a central registration facility, rather than being handled at individual schools. Centralization of intakes permitted extensive and efficient testing of language skills and identification of student needs, including noneducation matters such as medical issues and nutritional concerns. Grade-level and school placement decisions were based on these assessments.

Students enrolled in Fairfax's ESL program received intensive instruction each day in listening comprehension, speaking, reading, and writing from certified ESL teachers. The amount of time students spent each day learning English depended on their proficiency level. The needs of a foreign-born student who was illiterate in his native language were quite different from those of another foreign-born student who could read and write in her native language. When enough language minority students were enrolled in a particular school, their instruction in English could be provided on-site. Schools with low numbers of language minority students cooperated with neighboring schools to sponsor a single centrally located ESL program. Elementary and intermediate school students remained at their assigned school all day, while high school students were bused to ESL centers each morning. They returned to their home school for lunch and afternoon classes.

Having a nationally recognized ESL program, of course, did not free FCPS from the need for continuing program improvement. As the number of language minority students grew in the mid-'80s, program adjustments had to be made. In 1984 a report on Fairfax's ESL programs indicated various issues that needed to be addressed. Some of the county's more than 12,000 language minority students were being placed in standard courses before they had mastered English (Latimer, March 15, 1984). Rather than a "sink-or-swim" approach, the report called for more transitional classes for language minority students. In response to concerns expressed by some teachers that certain schools had too great a concentration of language minority students, the report assured readers that clustering these students in certain schools had no adverse effect on the regular instructional program. Such concerns, however, reflected a consistent theme in the history of program development in Fairfax County. New programs designed to address the special needs of a particular group were encouraged and supported only so long as they were not perceived to interfere with core programs.

Giving the gifted their due

In their various efforts to address the needs of minority, non-English-speaking, underachieving, and disabled students, Fairfax's education leaders were careful not to sacrifice programs for the county's brightest and most able students. Had they done so, it is unlikely that the highly educated majority of the county's patrons would have continually rallied to support public education. Unlike many other large school systems, Fairfax did not experience a significant exodus of gifted students to private and parochial schools in the '80s.

By the early '80s FCPS had developed well-regarded programs for gifted elementary and middle-school students. Once in high school, gifted students were expected to enroll in honors and Advanced Placement courses and possibly accelerate their progress toward graduation. What was lacking, though, was a school expressly designed for these students, a high school Harvard. In 1984 Fairfax school officials decided to create such a facility.

Ever alert for opportunities masquerading as problems, Fairfax leaders seized on the need to close a high school in the eastern part of the county in order to propose a specialty high school. By merging Jefferson High School with Annandale High School, the former facility would be available to house the Thomas Jefferson High School for Science and Technology. Only the promise of this new school prevented parents of Jefferson students from actively resisting the merger. Thomas Jefferson originally was planned as a regional magnet school for gifted students from all northern Virginia school systems, but when the Fairfax School Board finally approved the conversion of Jefferson High School, they balked at regionalizing the new school (Painton, June 29, 1984). School Board members worried that some gifted Fairfax students might be denied admission if the school opened its doors to other students.

When the Jefferson magnet school opened in August of 1985, it contained a wealth of special features provided by local businesses. AT&T sponsored the Telecommunications Laboratory, Hazleton Laboratories, Inc. the Life Sciences and Biotechnology Laboratory, Virginia Power the Energy and Engineering Science Laboratory, Honeywell, Inc. the Computer Systems Laboratory, and Atlantic Research Corporation the Material Science Laboratory. The cost of these state-of-the-art laboratories, which ranged from a quarter to a half million dollars, was covered in large part by business donations to the Fairfax County Public Schools Education Foundation. Of the new school, outgoing Superintendent Burkholder said,

> Our notion was one of not only providing the best kind of academic foundation in mathematics and basic sciences, but to provide laboratory experiences that emphasize the technological spinoff that has occurred as a result of the advancement of science. (Henderson, February 5, 1985)

From its inception, Thomas Jefferson attracted widespread student interest. Admission to the school was on a competitive basis, a policy that would generate considerable controversy in the years to come. Criticism came from advocates for minority students who claimed that certain minorities, particularly blacks, were underrepresented at the school. Similar criticisms had been aimed at Fairfax's earlier efforts to address the needs of gifted students.

Throughout the early '70s concerns had been expressed about the criteria and procedures used to screen students for gifted programs at the elementary level (Lamont, 2002). Some felt that the singular focus on conventional academic skills placed many minority students at a disadvantage when they tried to qualify for gifted programs. In the late '70s, Fairfax responded by developing and implementing the Multi-Dimensional Screening Device (Kashuda, 1979). The MDSD examined a range of indicators of giftedness, including intellectual ability, creative and productive thinking, prowess in the visual and performing arts, leadership qualities, abstract thinking, and talents associated with cultural heritage. To qualify for a gifted program, a student had to manifest 4 out of 10 characteristics of giftedness on the MDSD and pass a review by a committee of Fairfax educators.

During the early '80s, Fairfax began to focus its efforts in gifted education on the youngest students in the school system, those in kindergarten, first, and second grade. Previously Fairfax had concentrated on developing centers and school-based programs for the upper elementary grades and intermediate schools. By zeroing in on younger students, the school system hoped to increase minority participation in gifted programs. By the mid-'80s, Fairfax County Public Schools could boast of having one of the most comprehensive programs for gifted students in the nation.

A Good School System Keeps Getting Better

Shortly after Terrel H. Bell became Ronald Reagan's Secretary of Education, he addressed 700 Fairfax school administrators at Mount Vernon High School (Feinberg, August 7, 1982). Bell acknowledged that Fairfax County Public Schools was one of the greatest school systems in the nation, but he wondered whether the citizens of the county fully appreciated how outstanding a school system they had. In 1981 high school seniors from Fairfax County had the highest average scores in the Washington metropolitan area on the Scholastic Aptitude Tests, surpassing seniors from Montgomery County, Maryland, and Arlington, Virginia, for the first time. The week before Bell's address, the Virginia Department of Education had announced that Fairfax students outscored all other Virginia students on the state's standardized achievement tests. Many school systems are able to demonstrate progress during flush times, but only great school systems manage to improve performance despite a tight economy and related challenges. During the late '70s and early '80s, Fairfax educators faced growing tensions over resources between the School Board and the Board of Supervisors, community displeasure over school closings and changes in school boundaries, and demands for greater attention to the needs of minority students. Federal and state regulations increased, even as school aid dwindled. While enrollments dropped, the numbers of students with special needs, including language minority students and students eligible for special education services, climbed.

By the time Robert R. (Bud) Spillane took over the helm from William J. Burkholder on July 1, 1985, Fairfax County Public Schools could boast that its students scored well above national norms in reading and mathematics on standardized tests developed by Science Research Associates (SRA) (Cohn, June 6, 1985). The SRA tests were administered to students in the fourth, sixth, eighth, and eleventh grades. Whatever problems had caused Fairfax students to dip below national norms a decade earlier had been corrected. Possible contributors to improved test scores included newly initiated intermediate and high school reading centers and the establishment of computer-based Personalized Learning Plans (PLP) for struggling students who were not receiving special education services.

Why was Fairfax able to emerge from a difficult period stronger than ever? Among the key ingredients of success were (1) a willingness to seek out and address problems and (2) a commitment to finding and trying new ways to do things.

That Fairfax educators continually monitored the effectiveness of their programs was a function not only of a high level of professional concern, but also of a community heavily invested in seeing that its children received the best education possible. Black parents who left Washington, D.C. and other places to live in Fairfax County typically did so because of the school system's reputation for excellence. They were unwilling to accept large gaps in achievement between their children and white students. The same could be said for the growing numbers of immigrants who sought the American Dream south of the Potomac. Add to these voices those of affluent white parents who expected their children to get into the best colleges in the country, and it is easy to understand why complacency was not an option for Fairfax educators.

Fairfax's commitment to innovation was apparent in virtually everything the school system undertook. Fairfax educators could be counted on to keep track of the latest instructional practices and curriculum reforms. Fairfax programs designed to address students with special needs reflected the latest thinking, whether it concerned how to reach slow readers or how to accelerate learning for exceptionally gifted youngsters. Thomas Jefferson High School for Science and Technology, vocational centers, secondary reading centers, and the English as a Second Language program served as testimony to Fairfax's desire to deliver high quality, cutting edge educational opportunities for all students.

The organization and management of the school system also reflected Fairfax's commitment to innovation. To monitor and evaluate its steady stream of new programs, policies, and practices, Fairfax became one of the first school systems in Virginia to create a Division of Research and Testing (1976). The school system's trailblazing tendencies could be seen in its experimentation with Management by Objectives (MBO), program audits, zero-based budgeting, the design-build process for securing bids on new school construction, and state-of-the-art management information systems. To ensure that the voice of students reached the ears of division leaders, Fairfax established a countywide student advisory council in the '70s and provided for student representation on the School Board. To promote high quality instruction, Fairfax implemented peer evaluation and merit pay in the '80s. To encourage greater local participation in school improvement efforts, principals and teacher leaders were trained in site-based management.

When the National Commission on Excellence in Education issued its report on the state of American public schooling in 1983 and warned that "a rising tide of mediocrity" was threatening the nation and its people, Fairfax educators could feel, with ample justification, that the indictment had not been aimed at their school system. They had succeeded in creating a first-class school system and maintaining its reputation during trying times. The coming years would reveal whether or not they could sustain their success amidst challenges both new and familiar.

CHAPTER 3

Growing Bigger and More Diverse

The forces that have shaped and continue to influence public education in Fairfax County are no different than those that have affected most suburban school systems across the United States. The opening chapters focused on the pivotal roles of court decisions, demographics, and economics in the three decades following the Brown decision. From the mid-'80s through the first years of the new millennium, these factors continued to present major challenges for Fairfax educators. So, too, did the rise of partisan politics and the ever-expanding role of federal and state government in local education. The present chapter reviews changes in school enrollment in Fairfax County, especially the resumption of population growth and the increasing diversity of the student body, and the impact of these changes on school system programs and policies. Chapter 4 then examines the growing politicization of education in Fairfax, especially concerning school finances. From 1985 until 2004, Fairfax County, along with the rest of the United States, experienced two major periods of economic growth and two periods of sustained economic decline. How the school system responded to these shifts reveals a great deal about the changing politics of suburban education. Chapter 5 focuses on the impact of the accountability movement on Fairfax County Public Schools. First the state of Virginia and then the federal government launched initiatives designed to raise academic standards and promote educational accountability. In responding to these initiatives, Fairfax County educators demonstrated how an excellent school system can get even better.

While demographic changes, economic ups and downs, local politics, and government initiatives will be addressed somewhat independently, anyone familiar with public education realizes that these forces are highly interactive. When the number of students from poor families rises, for example, the demand for costly educational programs often increases without a commensurate expansion of the tax base. Complex decisions must be made about how to allocate limited educational resources. Politics comes into play, as special interest groups defend their pet programs against possible budget cuts. State and federal government may be called on to intervene when the interests of particular groups of students are considered to be at risk of inadequate funding and attention. Only by considering how these various forces have impacted Fairfax County Public Schools can we gain an understanding of the evolution of a suburban education empire.

Enrollment Growth, the Sequel

After a decade of declining school enrollments, Fairfax County's school-age population began to rise again in the fall of 1984, and it had not abated by 2004. The story of renewed growth, however, is not to be told in numbers alone, for many of the new students represented "nontraditional" groups. Addressing the varied educational needs of these newcomers has posed a number of challenges for Fairfax educators.

When Fairfax schools opened for the fall semester of 1987, they welcomed 3,000 new students, bringing total enrollment to nearly 131,000 students (Cohn, September 3, 1987). Fairfax had risen by this point to the rank of 10th largest school system in the United States. Having anticipated much of the surge, FCPS prepared to open six new schools—five elementary schools and one high school—the following year in the rapidly growing southern and western sectors of the county. It is worth noting that the new elementary schools were roughly twice the size of the previous generation of elementary schools. Over a million square feet of new school space—a record at the time—awaited Fairfax students in 1988. As the finishing touches were put on the six new schools, Superintendent Spillane readied a proposal to build five additional schools (Cohn, December 15, 1987).

The kind of growth experienced by Fairfax County, of course, cannot always be predicted with complete accuracy. Many students and parents suffered through overcrowding and anxieties concerning school boundary shifts, as they waited for new schools to be completed. By the fall of 1990 the steady increase in school-age population resulted in boundary-change proposals affecting 50

KEY DATES FOR FAIRFAX COUNTY PUBLIC SCHOOLS: 1986-1997

1986 Gifted program launched for students in grades K-2

1990 Consulting firm is hired to assess efforts by FCPS to raise minority achievement

1991 Consulting firm submits report on minority achievement

Superintendent Spillane develops proposal to raise minority achievement

School Board votes to create a magnet school at Bailey's Elementary School

1993 Special task force issues report on the needs of ESL students in FCPS

1997 Daniel Domenech appointed Superintendent

President Clinton cites Fairfax County as a model of what a community can do to accommodate diversity

---

of Fairfax's 156 schools, primarily in the northern and eastern sectors of the county, where growth had slowed or ceased altogether (Redding, November 15, 1990). While the primary goal of these proposals was stated, at least publicly, to be the relief of overcrowding, district officials acknowledged that a secondary aim was to distribute minority students more evenly among Fairfax schools. The importance of this aim was not universally acknowledged, however. One central office administrator acknowledged that charges of "social engineering" and "reverse discrimination" compelled FCPS to abandon any consideration of racial mix in the late '90s.

Despite concerns about overcrowding and redistricting, Fairfax County continued to be perceived as an attractive place to live and raise a family. In 1998 *Money* magazine ranked the Washington metropolitan area as the top place to live in the Northeast. Fueled by growth in the computer, electronics, and communications industries, the suburbs surrounding Washington, D.C. became a magnet for newcomers. Even when the high-tech "bubble" burst in 2000, Fairfax's population continued to grow, annually adding hundreds of new students to the school system. By 2003 the county topped one million residents, and Fairfax County Public Schools enrolled nearly 166,000 students. To relieve continued overcrowding, the school system was forced to utilize 750 trailers at an annual cost of $5 million in order to accommodate 13,800 students.

To appreciate the challenges presented by this growth, it is important to look at the changing make-up of Fairfax's students and their families. Fairfax's oldest minority group—African-Americans—continued to grow in numbers during the '80s and '90s. By 2001 FCPS enrolled 16,909 black students or 10.5 percent of the total school population, up from 8.4 percent in 1985 (Cohn, September 5, 1985; Seymour, April 28, 2002). Many of these black students came from well-to-do families, reflecting the fact that the Washington metropolitan area led the nation in African-American prosperity (Cohn and Keating, October 20, 2002). The 2000 Census revealed that blacks and whites in Fairfax, like many other suburban communities, were more likely than a decade earlier to go home to integrated neighborhoods. Hispanics, on the other hand, were more likely to live in ethnic enclaves (Cohen and Cohn, April 1, 2001). Improving economic circumstances and increased residential integration, however, did not eliminate the achievement gap between black and white students. Concerns also continued to be expressed about the underrepresentation of black students in programs for the gifted.

While the numbers of blacks in Fairfax rose during the last decades of the 20th century, the increase paled next to that of immigrants. During the 1990s, Fairfax County welcomed a staggering 112,841 immigrants ("By the Numbers," December 15, 2002). Herndon, a town in Fairfax County, illustrated this growth. In 1990, 1 out of every 10 Herndon residents was Hispanic. A decade later, one out of every four of Herndon's 22,000 residents was Hispanic (Whoriskey, April 26, 2001). The 2000 Census indicated that 237,677 of Fairfax's residents were foreign born ("By the Numbers," December 8, 2002). While Hispanics accounted for 31 percent of this number, the largest percentage of immigrants came from Asia. One of every two foreign-born residents of Fairfax County came from an Asian country (Whoriskey and Cohen, November 23, 2001). A language other than English was spoken in nearly 30 percent of the homes in the county. In 1996 the 10 languages, other than English, that were most frequently spoken by Fairfax students included the following (Seymour, June 13, 2002):

Spanish	5,036 students
Vietnamese	1,157 students
Korean	957 students

Urdu	392 students
Chinese	587 students
Arabic	371 students
Farsi	310 students
Japanese	201 students
Punjabi	134 students
Cambodian	121 students

By 2001, the order of most of the frequently spoken foreign languages along with the number of students speaking them had changed (Seymour, June 13, 2002):

Spanish	9,825
Korean	1,713
Urdu	1,004
Vietnamese	986
Arabic	771
Farsi/Persian	646
Chinese	460
Punjabi	220
Hindi	167
Somali	167

Concerned that its growing numbers of non-English and limited-English speakers would be unable to take advantage of local services, Fairfax County officials in the fall of 2002 created the position of language-access coordinator (Cho, November 17, 2002). This individual's charge was to find ways to communicate what the county had to offer to Fairfax's various language minorities. Meanwhile, Fairfax's adult education programs struggled to keep up with the demand for courses in English.

Along with changes in its cultural and linguistic makeup, Fairfax County has found itself changing economically. To be sure, it remains one of the nation's wealthiest jurisdictions. The median annual household income of $98,042 was the highest in the United States in 2001 (Bredemeier, November 26, 2001). The local economy in the same year was the Washington area's largest at 61.5 billion dollars. Local residents joked about getting Nordstrom's when they dialed 911. Amidst this affluence, however, were growing signs of economic disadvantage. Between 1990 and 1994, for example, the number of school-aged children in Fairfax whose household incomes fell below the federal poverty line rose 134 percent, from

5,099 to 11,955 (O'Harrow, May 10, 1997). This number represented approximately 8 percent of the school-aged population in
the county. Not surprisingly, many of the poor were Fairfax's most
recent arrivals.

So alarmed over the influx of poor people were Fairfax County
leaders that they reversed their position on affordable health care
centers, homeless shelters, and other programs for disadvantaged
residents. The threat of older neighborhoods, particularly those in
the eastern areas around Route 1 and Baileys Crossroads, becoming "overwhelmed by poverty" led local politicians in 1997 to cut
welfare benefits, block expansion of subsidized housing, and
tighten policies allowing unemployed persons access to public
housing (Lipton, June 29, 1997). Withdrawing the welcome mat for
poor people was justified on the grounds that there were insufficient resources to take care of all those individuals who already
resided in the county.

Despite these measures, the number of poor families continued
to rise. By the spring of 2001, 29,805 students, or 19 percent of
Fairfax's school-aged population, received free or reduced-price
school lunches (Benning, March 15, 2001). Two years later the
school system's website reported that 23 percent of its students
were eligible for free or reduced-price lunches. An estimated 2,000
county residents were listed as homeless (Benning, March 15,
2001). This figure represented a 25 percent jump from 1998, when
Fairfax first compiled data on homeless residents (Branigan and
Cho, March 5, 2002). The growing number of needy individuals
coupled with steadily rising population diversity gave suburban
Fairfax County an increasingly "urban" character as it entered the
21st century.

Several other demographic developments also are worth
noting. The 2000 Census indicated that slightly less than half of
Fairfax homeowners had lived in the same house for five years
("By the Numbers," November 24, 2002). Coupled with the large
number of transient renters, this statistic suggested that Fairfax
schools had to cope with significant numbers of students moving
into and out of their attendance zones each year. Of equal significance for FCPS was the rapid growth of nonfamily households in
the county. In 1990 married households with children outnum-
bered non-family households 90,762 to 78,798 (Cohn, February 6,
2002). A decade later, the gap had dwindled substantially (105,709

households with children to 100,433 nonfamily households). The *Washington Post* reporter who examined these figures suggested that greater conflict between couples with children and single adults over issues like school funding might lie ahead for Fairfax (Cohn, February 6, 2002).

Faced with familiar problems (rapidly expanding school-age population, achievement gap between black and white students) as well as a host of new challenges (significant numbers of recent immigrants and poor families), Fairfax County educators from the '80s into the new century refused to rest on their laurels or adopt a "this too shall pass" attitude regarding local changes. Instead they sought new ways to address the concerns of their neediest students while not forgetting their systemwide commitment to educational excellence. The following sections spotlight some of the ways the school system adjusted to shifting circumstances.

Narrowing the Gap

When the Fairfax School Board adopted its instructional priorities for 1984-1985, the list reflected an ambitious agenda for improvement. The nine priorities included the following (unordered in terms of importance):

- Integrate into all disciplines, K-12, critical thinking skills, study skills, and communication skills with primary emphasis on improving student writing skills.

- Strengthen the mathematics and science instructional programs.

- Continue the study of secondary school scheduling practices that hold promise for providing a challenging, enriched, and balanced curriculum for all students.

- Continue planning, implementing, and evaluating the program for gifted and talented students.

- Maintain efforts in the nonsmoking and substance-abuse awareness programs.

- Continue interagency efforts to address the mental health of troubled students.

- Develop and implement a plan to integrate and enrich the elementary curriculum.

- Provide for the continuous, systematic evaluation and improvement of selected educational programs at all levels.

- Develop alternatives for socially maladjusted students. (*Fairfax County Public Schools Bulletin*, October 1984, p. 4)

One goal, at least according to the thinking of School Board member Robert Frye, was conspicuously absent, however. No mention was made of addressing the academic needs of minority students. In June of 1984, the School Board corrected the omission and adopted a 10th priority:

- Improve the academic aspirations and achievement of minority students.

To provide the resources necessary to work on this priority, the School Board also added a new item to its list of "management priorities":

- Develop a plan for the differentiated allocation of resources to benefit students in schools with special needs.

Two key elements of a comprehensive initiative aimed at narrowing the achievement gap between white and black students thus were in place. They would remain so when Robert Spillane took over as Superintendent, though the wording of the instructional priority was modified. The school system's 1986-1987 Management Plan expressed the priority thusly:

- Improve the academic aspirations and achievement of all underachievers, with particular emphasis on underachieving minority students. (*Fairfax County Public Schools Bulletin*, August 1986, p. 5)

The same issue of the *Fairfax County Public Schools Bulletin* that listed the School Board priorities for Spillane's second year at the helm also summarized what had been done during the 1985-1986 school year to address minority student achievement. Eighteen different initiatives were noted, topped by the completion of the first *Annual Report on the Achievement and Aspirations of Minority Students in FCPS*. Other actions included the implementation of Project FAME—a program to increase the enrollment of females and minorities in high school mathematics and computer science; a review of minority representation in high school programs for gifted and talented students; inservice training on strategies for working with families of minority students; and the addition of four new Head Start classrooms. To facilitate the continuous monitoring of minority student achievement, the district developed a "Resource Notebook for School-based Evaluation." With the help of teachers and community members, every principal was expected to develop and implement a school improvement plan that addressed the achievement and aspirations of minority students. It is important to note that these initiatives were intended to assist all minorities, not just African Americans.

When standardized test results for Fairfax students were published at the beginning of the 1985-86 school year, it became clear that only a sustained effort over many years would narrow the achievement gap. Overnight miracles were unlikely. Black students trailed white students by as much as 36 percentile points on the Science Research Associates (SRA) tests (Cohn, September 5, 1985). While white students scored about the 80th percentile, black students scored around the 50th percentile, the national midpoint. Fairfax dedicated over $2 million in the 1985-86 school year alone to address minority achievement. Most of the money was earmarked to hire more teachers and support staff in 22 elementary schools with high numbers of minority and poor students.

By the fall of 1989, Fairfax school officials had begun to see some modest benefits from their investment in raising minority achievement. Black, Hispanic, and Asian students who had spent 5 or more years in Fairfax schools performed significantly better on standardized tests than more recent arrivals (Baker, December 7, 1989). This finding suggested that prolonged exposure to Fairfax teachers and programs made a difference. Of the three largest minority groups, however, black students showed the smallest benefit from length of time in Fairfax schools. What was more alarming was the persistent gap in achievement between white and minority students. Despite the fact that black enrollment in gifted and talented classes had jumped from 8.5 percent in 1985 to 14.1 percent by 1989, and black enrollment in upper-level science classes had climbed over the same period from 13 percent to 22 percent, the gap in standardized test scores between white and black students still ranged from 26 to 35 points (Baker, December 7, 1989).

Superintendent Spillane increasingly found himself at the center of controversy over the continuing achievement gap. When he failed to show up at the initial presentation of test data mentioned in the preceding paragraph, a local black leader chided him. Others criticized him for allowing the initiative to improve black achievement to slip from its previous high priority status (Baker, March 6, 1990). When a district plan to operate 30 summer school enrichment programs for underachieving students was scaled back to 12 programs, Spillane drew additional fire. The tension between the Superintendent and the black community grew so heated that some black leaders called for Spillane to resign if the achievement of black students was not improved.

To address the growing concerns of the black community, Fairfax officials hired former Washington, D.C., Superintendent Floretta McKenzie in the fall of 1990. Her charge was to assess the school system's 6-year-old effort to raise minority achievement. Spillane's original preference for an in-house study had been rejected by School Board member Robert Frye, who believed that only an outsider could get to the heart of the issue (Baker, October 11, 1990).

When the McKenzie report was presented to the School Board on May 15, 1991, there was little about which Fairfax educators could exult. The school system's campaign to address minority achievement was criticized for being fragmented, lacking accountability, and relying too much on "gimmicks" (Baker, May 16, 1991). Despite the existence of a Minority Student Achievement Office in the central administration and the allocation of special resources to schools with large numbers of minority students, minority students continued to be more likely to drop out, be retained at grade level, score lower on standardized tests, and receive low grades. The report claimed that Fairfax's highly touted programs and centers for gifted students were elitist. It recommended that the Minority Student Achievement Office be expanded and granted greater authority, recruitment efforts to obtain more minority teachers be stepped up, and specific improvement targets for minority achievement be set. These targets should become, according to the report, a primary basis for evaluating principals and teachers.

Five months after the McKenzie Report was presented, Spillane submitted to the School Board a proposal to improve the academic achievement of minority students (Brown, October 3, 1991). Despite deteriorating economic conditions, he recommended allocating an extra $1.7 million annually to reducing first grade class sizes and expanding special reading programs. Pupil-teachers ratios would be lowered from 24-to-1 to 15-to-1 in the first grade classes of 29 elementary schools with high concentrations of low-achieving students.

By the time the School Board voted on Spillane's proposal in December, the budget situation in Fairfax County was being compared to the Great Depression (Brown, December 6, 1991). Instead of $1.7 million for 29 schools, the School Board only approved $500,000 to reduce first grade class size in 15 schools.

Efforts to narrow the achievement gap continued throughout the '90s. As the economy perked up, additional funds were dedicated to the cause. As long as the performance of *all* minority students was aggregated, Fairfax officials were able to report steady progress. When the achievement of black and Hispanic students was disaggregated, however, results continued to be disappointing. Just before the opening of the new school year in 1998, the school system reported that 38 percent of African American students and 37 percent of Hispanic students averaged less than a C grade in high school. The figures were almost as bad for middle schoolers. Robert Frye, vice chairman of the School Board and the person who had requested the information on grades, found the news "appalling" (Benning, August 7, 1998). He was especially concerned that the two high schools with the worst performance by black and Hispanic students were South Lakes High School and Madison High School, schools located in relatively affluent parts of the county.

It is tempting to cite Fairfax's lack of success in narrowing the achievement gap between white and black students as evidence that the school system's vaunted reputation for educational excellence was overblown. If some black students lagged behind their white peers, however, it was not because the school system had ignored their plight. To some extent the issue of African American academic achievement probably cannot be fully understood by studying only one school system.

In 1997, when John Ogbu (2003) studied African American achievement in Shaker Heights, Ohio, an affluent suburb of Cleveland, he found a pattern of low academic performance similar to that in Fairfax. Ogbu argued that the persistence of low performance among significant numbers of relatively well-to-do black students could not be attributed solely to school-based factors ("the system"). Blame, he contended, must also be laid at the doorstep of

the African American community and its beliefs about the instrumental value of school credentials and the particular strategies
needed by black students to cope with school (Ogbu, 2003, pp. 52-
54). Ogbu noted that many other minority groups have managed to
succeed in public schools, even when English was not their native
language, because community factors were aligned to support educational success.

Despite the lack of significant improvements, Fairfax educators persisted in their efforts to address minority achievement.
When Dan Domenech succeeded Bud Spillane in January of 1997,
he intensified efforts to narrow the achievement gap. Some of his
initiatives dovetailed with the school system's campaign to address
Virginia's new educational accountability program. A discussion of
these efforts will be presented in chapter 5. Domenech, himself a
Cuban-born immigrant, expressed his determination to increase
the percentage of minority students in gifted programs, Advanced
Placement courses, and Thomas Jefferson High School for Science
and Technology. Domenech's commitment began to pay dividends
almost immediately. By the fall of 2002, Fairfax officials boasted
that the number of black students in gifted programs had risen 41
percent since the new Superintendent took office (Seymour, July 3,
2002). The scores of black students on Virginia's Standards of
Learning tests rose on 22 of the 28 tests given in May of 2002
(Helderman, October 24, 2002).

Integrating Fairfax's Foreign-born Newcomers

What had begun as a trickle of immigrants in the late '60s
became a flood by the late '80s. Some newcomers to FCPS came
from highly educated and well-to-do families. Others were poor
and illiterate in their native language. Addressing the varying
educational needs of this diverse collection of new students put
Fairfax educators to the test.

The school system's solid commitment to English as a Second
Language (ESL) programs showed no signs of abating as the tide of
newcomers rose. By the beginning of the fall semester in 1985,
FCPS enrolled approximately 3,800 students in ESL classes
(Hochman, July 9, 1985). Fairfax ESL teachers never spoke to students in their native language, opting instead to rely on books with
word-picture diagrams, filmstrips, flashcards, charts, charades, and

continual repetition. Outside critics claimed that the early success of Fairfax's ESL programs could be attributed to the relatively high socioeconomic status of immigrants to northern Virginia. They predicted that the ESL approach was less likely to succeed with the burgeoning numbers of poor and uneducated immigrants.

Not inclined to take any of its programs' effectiveness for granted, Fairfax County Public Schools' officials instructed ESL staff to conduct a thorough examination of their offerings in 1989 ("Executive Summary, ESL Task Force Report," March 9, 1993). The eventual result was a variety of new initiatives, including a switch from center-based to school-based programs, a special literacy program for students with little or no previous schooling, an alternative high school for ESL students aged 17 to 20 years of age, and new assessment procedures for gathering data on ESL students. It appeared that Fairfax had risen to the challenge of a rapidly increasing immigrant population. Then came the McKenzie Report in the spring of 1991.

The McKenzie Report examined all minorities, not only African Americans. It was highly critical of the narrow aims of the school system's ESL program. The major thrust of criticism was that language-minority students spent so much time on basic skills that they had little opportunity to undertake the academic work needed to prepare for college (Baker, May 16, 1991). As a consequence, many older ESL students were counseled to drop out and take adult education classes or transfer to nearby schools in Alexandria or Arlington, where they were more likely to receive academic instruction. The immigrant group that experienced the most difficulties was Hispanic students. They were as likely to test poorly and repeat a grade as African American students. Part of the problem, according to the McKenzie Report, was the fact that only 1.2 percent of Fairfax teachers were Hispanic, and bilingual guidance counselors were virtually nonexistent.

Two months after receiving the McKenzie Report and its accompanying negative publicity, the School Board approved an initiative aimed at helping immigrant students with little prior education to earn a high school diploma (Baker, July 26, 1991). By this time Fairfax's ESL population had mushroomed to almost 6,700 students. To address the needs of the least-educated ESL students, special academic classes were initiated so that they would not be compelled to dive immediately into regular science, history, and other core subjects. Reflecting Fairfax's preferred prescription for reform, the new classes were first piloted in five high schools and subsequently expanded, based on an assessment of their effectiveness.

In the spring of 1992, an ESL Task Force made up of Fairfax educators and community members was convened to review the K-12 ESL instructional program, assess its strengths and weaknesses, investigate alternative instructional models, and make recommendations on how better to meet the needs of ESL students. The Task Force grew out of the McKenzie Report's call for a comprehensive review of all programs and policies for language minority students. Meeting twice monthly for a year, the ESL Task Force focused on eight aspects of the ESL program: staff development, curriculum, kindergarten and preschool programs, gifted and talented programs, special education, evaluation, parents and guardians, and general procedures ("Executive Summary, ESL Task Force Report," March 9, 1993). To the extent that most of the Task Force's recommendations called for expanding or institutionalizing existing programs and practices, the report was a ringing endorsement for Fairfax's overall approach to language minority instruction. The Task Force did note, though, that the amount spent on each Fairfax ESL student—$1,054—was considerably less than that spent by neighboring Arlington ($1,851), Alexandria ($2,132), and Prince William County ($2,259).

When school opened in September of 1993, it was clear that the challenge of educating language minority students was not going to disappear. A staff writer for the *Washington Post* provided an extensive description of Fairfax's newest residents (O'Harrow, September 2, 1993). Representing 187 countries and more than 100 languages, students for whom English was not their native language made up 16 percent of the student population of FCPS. ESL classes were offered in 110 schools, more than half of all Fairfax schools and special education centers. To instruct language minority students, Fairfax employed 260 ESL teachers. Translators were called on to tape phone messages, translate school communications, interpret parent concerns, and assist in diagnostic testing. FAST Math, a federally funded program for immigrant children with little formal schooling, was available in some high schools, middle schools, and for the first time, at the elementary level. In a significant policy change, Fairfax planned to permit students to earn high school graduation credits for mathematics, science, and social studies classes taught through the ESL program. The article in *The Washington Post* indicated that this move was criticized by some people, who claimed academic standards would be lowered. Along with efforts to provide direct help to language minority students, Fairfax also forged ahead with multicultural instruction intended to raise awareness of different cultures among all students and promote greater sensitivity to cross-cultural differences.

One of Fairfax's most innovative responses to its increasingly diverse population was Bailey's Elementary School for the Arts and Sciences. Born amidst the turmoil of redistricting in the early '90s, the elementary magnet was the school system's answer to sensitive boundary change problems (Baker, March 7, 1991). As immigrants poured into certain neighborhoods, some nonimmigrant parents expressed concerns regarding the schools to which their children were assigned. Fears ranged from lower academic expectations to student safety. Redrawing attendance areas for schools already was a highly controversial process in Fairfax, one that was sure to bring out parents in droves. Caught in the crossfire was Bailey's Elementary School, located in a neighborhood made up primarily of recently arrived Hispanic and Asian immigrants. In 1991, 81 percent of Bailey's students spoke a native language other than English. Local PTA leaders pressed the School Board to transfer more native English-speaking students to Bailey's in order to achieve better ethnic balance and provide more peer role models. They even threatened to sue the school system if it failed to act on their demands. When the parents of students who would be reassigned to Bailey's got wind that the Superintendent was considering the move, however, they protested strongly.

In an effort to placate both sides, the School Board voted on March 7, 1991, to convert Bailey's to a magnet school and offer special programs that would be sufficiently attractive to lure English-speaking students on a voluntary basis (Heath, March 8, 1991). Efforts to proceed with plans for the magnet program temporarily stalled over budget issues, but the delay finally ended when the Bailey's PTA again threatened to sue the School Board. Noting that there was not one native English-speaking student in the entire fifth grade, the PTA President argued that FCPS was supporting segregationist policies by not appropriating funds to implement the magnet school design (Duckworth, 1995). The School Board approved $2.3 million to phase in science and arts programs over the three-year period from 1992 to 1995. When the first lottery was held for children outside of the Bailey's attendance area, 300 applicants vied for 85 openings.

Bailey's Elementary School for the Arts and Sciences has become a remarkable experiment in learning. The school boasts a performing arts program anchored by a specially constructed black box theater, a technology lab with 25 computer stations staffed by a full-time teacher and assistant, a science lab replete with microscopes and aquariums, a communications lab with video production studio, and an electronic music lab. Partnerships with the Smithsonian Institution, the U.S. Forest Service, and Thomas Jefferson High School for Science and Technology have led to a museum-in-the-school initiative, special field trips, and a tutoring program. Other unique learning opportunities include a Spanish partial immersion program, FAST Math, Reading Recovery, before-and after-school child care, a community room to accommodate parent liaisons, and a special homework center sponsored by the Police Department. It would be difficult to find a more impressive showcase of what a school system can do to promote cultural awareness and integration while also providing outstanding opportunities for the academic growth of all students.

Initiatives such as Bailey's Elementary School for the Arts and Sciences and the use of panels of immigrant parents to raise Fairfax educators' awareness of cultural differences have attracted considerable attention. In the fall of 1997, President Clinton cited Fairfax County as a glowing example of what a community can do to accommodate diversity (Baker, October 1, 1997). Clinton's claim that Fairfax County Public Schools was the most diverse school system in the United States placed the division squarely in the national spotlight. Interestingly, spokespersons for Fairfax responded to the president's remarks by moderating the perception that the school system was an exemplar. Perhaps to avoid the curse of inflated publicity or simply out of an honest appraisal of work yet to be done, they reminded people that the county had experienced its share of "racially charged disputes over police behavior, school boundaries and government hiring" (Baker, October 1, 1997).

Fairfax's language minority population continued to grow through the '90s and into the new century, but the school system's commitment to ESL never wavered, even when its neighbors embraced bilingual education. Fairfax's highly regarded programs for immigrant students would face new challenges, as accountability initiatives and high-stakes testing, first from the state and later from the federal government, were implemented in the late '90s and early years of the new century. Chapter 5 examines how FCPS accommodated these new developments.

A System within a System

English as a Second Language programs and initiatives aimed at closing the achievement gap between white and minority students have been and continue to be substantial undertakings for Fairfax County Public Schools, but they are only several elements of a vast system within a system designed to educate a variety of needy students. By the time the term "at-risk student" became popular in the mid-'80s, FCPS already boasted an extensive network of special education centers and programs, and school officials were beginning to consider alternatives for struggling students who were not covered by the special education umbrella. The school system's 1983-84 Management Plan for the first time included a separate heading for "alternative programs." The initial goal for this category involved establishing a task force to explore "the feasibility of alternative programs for socially maladjusted students whose needs are not addressed by special programs" (*Fairfax County Public Schools Bulletin*, August 1984, p. 11). Following the task force's report, visits were made to alternative programs in other school systems and a plan to implement task force recommendations was drafted. The beginning phase of the plan involved inservice training and designing an Alternative Education Center for intermediate-age "socially maladjusted" students.

By the time the 1989-90 Management Plan was approved, "alternative programs" had been replaced as a heading by "students at risk," and this category of school system goals had been moved from the section on "instructional programs" to the section on "community interaction." Reporting on progress related to "students at risk," the August 1989 *Bulletin* for FCPS noted the implementation of Reading Recovery, an early intervention program that reduced reading failure for first graders; the expansion of the Accelerated Learning program, a summer-school intervention for low-performing students in reading and mathematics; and the proliferation of mentoring programs, including Females Achieving Mathematics Equity (FAME), a summer program in which minority eighth grade girls shadowed women in math-related careers. School system targets for 1990-1991 included developing and implementing a countywide dropout prevention program that encompassed a data management system, inservice training, and a targeted follow-up for every student designated as a dropout during 1988-1989. Improving the tracking of at-risk students and ensuring that they did not become "lost" became a consistent theme for Fairfax, as it struggled to overcome the challenges of high student mobility and the school system's huge size and organizational complexity.

"Students at risk" disappeared as a category for objectives in the 1991-92 Annual Operating Plan. Instead, objectives related to needy students were clustered in the section on "instructional programs" under such headings as "early intervention" and "racial, ethnic, and language minority students." Many of the objectives derived from recommendations in the McKenzie Report. It is worth noting that the annual goals guiding the allocation of resources and personnel in Fairfax have vacillated between treating all needy students as one group and differentiating between African American students, language minority students, and other students at risk. The perceived costs and benefits of lumping together all struggling students apparently have varied over time.

The variety of opportunities available to Fairfax students who have been unable or unwilling to take advantage of regular education programs is enormous. Special education constitutes the largest element of this system within a system. In 2003 Fairfax operated 25 special services centers, including 17 centers for students with emotional disabilities, 2 centers for hearing-impaired students, 2 centers for students with physical disabilities, 2 centers for students with moderate retardation and severe disabilities, and 2 career centers.[1] Preschool Diagnostic Centers were available at 2 locations to provide comprehensive developmental assessments for children between the ages of 2 and 5 years. Diagnostic teams consisting of various specialists made recommendations for children who exhibited significant developmental delays and therefore qualified for special education services prior to entering kindergarten.

In recent years, Fairfax's policy has been to accommodate the needs of as many special education students as possible in classrooms with nondisabled students. The success of this commitment is revealed by the fact that, in 2003, 92 percent of high school students with disabilities graduated with regular diplomas. Three out of five of these graduates went on to enroll in a postsecondary educational institution.

In addition to special education centers and programs, FCPS offers a comprehensive continuum of alternative education, ranging from schools for students who have been expelled or placed on long-term suspension to interagency operations for young people in the juvenile justice system to GED programs for students unable to earn a regular diploma. Fairfax operates four alternative high schools for students requiring a nontraditional learning environment in order to graduate. These open enrollment facilities provide classes from 8 a.m. to 9 p.m., thereby enabling students to hold a job or handle child care responsibilities while completing coursework. Courses are scheduled so that students, especially those with serious credit deficits, can complete a year's worth of academic work in a semester. The alternative high schools also operate year round, so that students also can make up work during the summer.

One of Fairfax's most innovative alternative high school programs was launched in the fall of 1994. The Landmark Shopping Center, near Alexandria, donated 3,700 square feet of commercial space to FCPS in order for the school system to create the Landmark Career Academy. Designed for noncollege-bound students, the academy allows students to complete their diploma work while simultaneously acquiring entry-level job skills. The shopping mall location makes it easier for students to complete the required 160-hour internship.

The Landmark Career Academy is just one of a variety of options designed to prepare Fairfax students for the world of work. The key to many of these programs' success is the collaborative arrangement between FCPS and local businesses. Retail and fashion marketing experience is available in classroom-on-the-mall programs at three local shopping complexes besides Landmark. Hotel management classes are offered at four Fairfax hotels. Project Opportunity is a high school completion program for students between the ages of 16 and 21 who are pregnant or parenting.

The latest additions to Fairfax's career development opportunities are its five high school academies. Each academy provides juniors and seniors with focused learning related to particular employment fields. Engineering and scientific technology programs are available at Chantilly, Edison, and Marshall High Schools. Health and human services are the focus at Chantilly and West Potomac High Schools. Other areas of concentration include international studies and business, and communications and the arts. Students enrolled in academy programs shadow workers, receive assistance from mentors, and participate in field-based internships. The list of programs available at the Chantilly Academy suggests the wide range of possible career development paths open to Fairfax students:

Advanced drawing	Dental careers
Air Force JROTC	Early childhood careers
Animal science	Electrical construction/engineering
Auto body	Engineering physics
Auto technology	Engineering systems
Basic technical drawing	Hotel management
Computer systems technology	Medical health technologies
Construction technologies	Network administration
Cosmetology	Network design and engineering
Criminal justice	Physics of technology
Culinary arts	

Placement options also exist for students who have gotten into disciplinary difficulties. The Alternative Learning Centers (ALC) are designed for students in grades 6 through 10 who have been involved in serious disciplinary incidents. ALC students focus on core academic courses and behavior improvement. Reentry to a base school is possible for students who demonstrate appropriate behavior and keep up with their coursework. A second disciplinary option located at selected Fairfax schools is the SUMMIT program (previously known as the Intervention and Support Program). Students in grades 3 through 11 whose behavior prevents other students from learning may be referred to a self-contained SUMMIT classroom, where they must complete academic assignments while also undertaking a behavior improvement plan. SUMMIT guidance counselors teach daily lessons covering such subjects as anger management, communication skills, behavioral ownership, and trust. Those who successfully complete their SUMMIT requirements can petition for reinstatement to their former school or an alternative program. Besides ALCs and SUMMIT classes, Fairfax also operates intervention seminars for students who have been suspended from school for violations of alcohol, drug, and tobacco policies.

Fairfax's Continuing Commitment to High-achieving Students

Had Fairfax County educators allowed opportunities for college-bound and gifted students to dwindle, as efforts to assist underachieving and at-risk students expanded, it is unlikely that the school system would be hailed today as a top performer.

Despite periodic budget crises and political battles over programs deemed to be elitist by critics, the School Board and top administrators maintained a steadfast commitment to providing and protecting challenging academic programs for Fairfax's large population of high achievers.

Continuing an initiative launched prior to his arrival, Bud Spillane oversaw the implementation of a gifted and talented program for students in grades K-2. Aligned with Virginia's Plan for the Gifted, the early elementary program sought to identify exceptional abilities in *all* children (*Fairfax County Public Schools Bulletin*, October 1986, p. 8). For each grade level, nine lessons designed to encourage critical and creative thinking and permit teachers to assess behaviors characteristic of gifted children were created. The K-2 program was piloted at eight elementary schools in the 1986-87 school year and subsequently expanded to all elementary schools. At the high school level, a special foreign language component for gifted students was introduced in the fall of 1986. The new course of studies in foreign languages complimented existing gifted programs in other core academic subjects.

No sooner had the new K-2 program been piloted than concerns were voiced about low minority participation in Fairfax's various gifted and talented offerings. On May 22, 1986, the countywide Human Relations Advisory Committee issued a report in which it noted that "inadequate numbers of intellectually gifted minorities" were being identified (McClain, 2001). Blame, in part, was directed at the screening test, a test that had not been normed for blacks and Hispanics. The test, according to the report, should not be used as the sole basis for placement in an elementary gifted center. The committee also called for a better effort to disseminate information on gifted programs to minority parents.

Progress toward greater minority participation in gifted programs was not immediate. In 1987-88 the *Annual Report on the Achievement and Aspirations of Minority Students in the Fairfax County Public Schools* indicated that the student population of elementary gifted centers was made up of 90.3 percent white, 2.0 percent black, 1.1 percent Hispanic, and 6.5 percent Asian students. At the time, blacks made up 9 percent, Hispanics 4.5 percent, and Asians 10.0 percent of the school system's total enrollment. Ensuring that all racial and ethnic groups shared in the benefits of Fairfax's most challenging academic programs remained a "front burner" issue for educators into the next century.

Nowhere was access to gifted programs a greater focus of concern than Thomas Jefferson High School for Science and Technology. Each year when school opened in September, the predictable scrutiny of the makeup of Jefferson's student body took place, and each year advocates for minority students voiced their disappointment. When Dan Domenech inherited the issue from his predecessor, he decided to try a new tack. Faced with the news in the fall of 2001 that Jefferson's freshman class contained only 2 black and 7 Hispanic students out of 420 students, he vowed to adopt a new selection process (Seymour, September 27, 2001). What was particularly alarming was not just the low number of minority freshmen, but the trend. Since 1997 the number of black freshmen at Jefferson had plummeted 92 percent. Hispanic freshmen dropped by 71 percent. A variety of reasons were offered for the drop-off—under-representation of minorities in elementary and middle school gifted programs, the reluctance of middle schoolers to leave their neighborhood school for specialty programs, and the demise of Fairfax's Visions program (Seymour, September 27, 2001). Visions had been a successful mathematics and science enrichment program for Fairfax minorities, but the program was axed in 1999, when several federal court rulings challenged minority-exclusive programs funded by public resources.

Domenech quickly learned how nonminority parents felt about his pledge to increase minority admission to Jefferson. Inundated by e-mails critical of his proposal to "guarantee" a certain number of slots for underrepresented groups, he was compelled to abandon his original proposal (Seymour, October 11, 2001; Seymour, October 18, 2001). Instead of allocating freshman slots by geographical area, a strategy that was certain to boost minority participation, Domenech's revised recommendation was to use traditional selection criteria to choose 400 new students each year and reserve the last 20 slots for underrepresented neighborhoods.

Why parents should have felt so strongly about admission to Jefferson was hardly a mystery. Annually boasting more National Merit Scholars and admissions offers from Ivy League colleges than any other public high school in the United States, selection for Jefferson was as close to a guarantee of academic success as a student could hope for. At what other public high school could students have access to college-caliber instruction and multimillion dollar technology, including a Cray supercomputer? Parents of Fairfax eighth graders were so anxious to get their children into

Jefferson that they enrolled them in expensive private programs to prepare them for the Jefferson entrance examination (Seymour, December 1, 2001). Some parents even relocated in order to send their children to middle schools with better track records for admission to Jefferson. A record 2,884 eighth graders sat for the entrance examination in December of 2001.

The following spring the number of African American and Hispanic students invited to attend Jefferson climbed to 30, a jump of 21 from the preceding year. Many of these students may have benefited from several new initiatives intended to boost minority representation. All Jefferson applicants, for example, received a test preparation booklet to help them study for the entrance examination. Jefferson's Parent-Teacher-Student Association (PTSA) diversity committee hosted a reception for all minority applicants and organized several test preparation courses. Despite the increased minority enrollment, a local advocate for minority students reminded school officials that one-quarter of Fairfax's eighth grade population consisted of minority students (Seymour, April 9, 2002). If they were chosen in proportion to their numbers, 105 minority students would have been admitted to Jefferson.

Based on the popularity of private test preparation courses and those organized by the Jefferson PTSA, the school system decided to sponsor its own test preparation program. Intended to encourage more minority students to consider attending Jefferson, the after-school pilot program attracted targeted students as planned, but it also attracted huge numbers of nonminority students as well. Unable to limit participation only to minority students, Fairfax discovered that its well-intentioned gesture actually benefited groups already well represented at Jefferson (Seymour, October 19, 2002). Controversy regarding admission to Jefferson surfaced again in the spring of 2003, when a local law professor published an article claiming that Jefferson discriminated against white students by "admitting the largest number of black students available" (Kalita, April 2, 2003). The professor examined the records of admitted black students and discovered that some of them had lower entrance examination scores than white students who were rejected. Few were surprised to learn that one of the rejected white students was the law professor's own child.

Thomas Jefferson was back in the spotlight in August, when Isis Castro, the outgoing chair of the School Board and Virginia's first elected Hispanic official, declared her frustration over the fact that only 40 of Jefferson's 1,689 students were Hispanic (Kalita, August 9, 2003). Castro suggested that a different method of identifying students was needed. Her recommendation is likely to receive consideration in light of the U.S. Supreme Court's ruling in June of 2003 that the University of Michigan can take race into account when deciding on which students to admit.

So much publicity has surrounded Thomas Jefferson High School for Science and Technology that it is easy to lose sight of all the other opportunities available to Fairfax's most capable students. Jefferson may be the brightest jewel in the crown, but it is certainly not the only one. The handbook describing Fairfax's special academic programs reveals a rich array of offerings for high achievers. All Fairfax high schools, for example, offer Advanced Placement courses, and 15 of the high schools allow students to undertake the Advanced Placement diploma program. Eight high schools operate the International Baccalaureate (IB) program for 11th and 12th graders. In order to earn a full IB diploma, students must pass external examinations in six subjects, participate in community service projects, and complete a 4,000 word essay. Unlike Jefferson and the gifted centers for elementary and middle school students, the rigorous IB program is open to all students. Several Fairfax middle schools are affiliated with the IB Middle Years program.

Fairfax officials express great pride in the fact that an advanced curriculum, either based on Advanced Placement courses or the International Baccalaureate program, is available to every student in every one of its 21 high schools and 3 secondary schools. They claim that Fairfax is the only large school system in the United States with such extensive access to challenging coursework. To reduce the likelihood that AP and IB courses become havens for select groups of students, enrollment is open to all students. What makes the open enrollment policy particularly meaningful is Superintendent Domenech's insistence that *every* student enrolled in an AP or IB course must take the external examination tied to that course. As a result, teachers cannot single out their highest-achieving students to take external examinations. Every AP and IB teacher is held accountable for teaching every one of their students. Teachers' evaluations are based, in part, on how well each of their students does on the AP and IB examinations. When *Newsweek* ("The Top High Schools," 2003) published its list of the best high schools in the U.S., 14 Fairfax high schools were listed among the top 150.[2]

Ninth and 10th grade students in Fairfax have access to pre-IB, honors, and gifted courses in English, mathematics, science, and social studies. By partnering with George Mason University, FCPS has developed the Early Identification Program (EIP) to provide middle and high school students from "traditionally underrepresented populations" with special opportunities to prepare for college. Contributions from the local business community have allowed Fairfax to offer high-achieving minority students in grades 6-8 the QUEST program. Students in QUEST receive three years of interdisciplinary, science-oriented instruction plus a host of enrichment opportunities, including field trips, special presentations, and access to the latest technology. Partial language immersion programs in French, German, Japanese, and Spanish are available at selected elementary and middle schools. Students participating in these programs are able to study various subjects from the regular curriculum in a foreign language. Arabic is now available to students in three Fairfax high schools. The success of Bailey's Elementary School for the Arts and Sciences led FCPS to create a second elementary magnet program, modeled after Bailey's, at Hunters Wood Elementary. Besides gifted centers for eligible students in grades 3 through 8, Fairfax also operates school-based gifted programs.

When Dan Domenech became Superintendent in 1997, some observers anticipated changes in Fairfax's approach to educating high-achieving students (McClain, 2001). The School Board adopted a new vision and mission statement for the school system that seemed to signal a commitment to expand access to challenging learning opportunities. The statement read as follows:

> The vision of Fairfax County Public Schools is to provide a gifted-quality education to every child in an instructional setting appropriate for his or her need. This vision is supported by a mission to educate all students to meet high academic standards and to prepare all students to be responsible citizens in the 21st century.

At least one mechanism for pursuing the new vision for "a gifted-quality education" for every student already was in place in the form of the Schoolwide Achievement Model (SAM). Launched on a pilot basis during Spillane's tenure, the SAM was designed to identify and address talents in *all* students. Funds, however, were not appropriated by the School Board to increase the number of schools involved in the initiative. Another indication that some anticipated changes under Domenech might be slow to materialize was the continuation of gifted centers. While Fairfax began to shift many students from ESL and special education centers to their neighborhood schools, no comparable transfers were made from gifted centers. Enrollment at gifted centers, in fact, has continued to grow with the overall student population. By the spring of 2001, the center enrollment for grades 3-8 stood at 4,290 students, or 6.5 percent of the population (McClain, 2001). Besides the open enrollment policy for AP and IB courses mentioned previously, a major shift related to gifted education that occurred under Domenech was administrative in nature. Gifted education was switched from the Department of Special Services and Special Education, where it had been located since the '70s, to the Instructional Services Department. Furthermore, oversight for elementary and middle school gifted education was divided between the directors of elementary and middle school programs.

That Fairfax County Public Schools has been able to balance its efforts to address the needs of various groups of students, from recently arrived immigrants to students with off-the-charts talent, is testimony to the flexibility and responsiveness of Fairfax educators. It also reflects a community with deep pockets and a penchant for politicizing the needs of its students. As will be seen in the next chapter, however, the community's generosity is not limitless, and educational politics can become bogged down in partisan bickering.

CHAPTER 4

The Intensification of Educational Politics

Historians of public education in the United States are fond of reminding people that politics and education have shared the same bed for well over a century. What is arguably unique to the past few decades, however, is the expansion and intensification of educational politics. Nowhere has this trend been more evident than in Fairfax County. Most of the individuals interviewed for this book commented on the proliferation of special interest groups and the prevalence of partisanship on virtually every issue facing the school system. No longer can school system leaders count on a reasonable level of agreement when changes are proposed. Most reform initiatives bring out well-organized groups of advocates and opponents. Some observers believe that the primary victim of increased politicization has been an overarching sense of the common good. No matter what the proposal for educational improvement, Fairfax educators know they will hear complaints ranging from inequity to excessive cost.

In no area of school operations has the mounting contentiousness been more evident than finance. When coffers are full, school systems may be able to placate most groups making educational demands, but when resources dry up and cuts must be made, educators quickly get a lesson in who has political influence and who doesn't. The history of merit pay in FCPS provides a useful example of the interplay of local politics and economics. Chapter 4 begins by tracing the rise of merit pay and the subsequent impact of the economic downturn of the early '90s. The next section looks in greater detail at how the Fairfax School Board confronted retrenchment during the period from 1991 through 1992. Budget problems surfaced again in the new millennium, but this time the School Board members who had to decide what to cut were elected instead of appointed, as their predecessors had been. The chapter examines how an elected School Board dealt with financial challenges and whether its response was significantly different from that of appointed School Boards. Not all examples of the heightened inter-mingling of politics and education in Fairfax County necessarily involve financial matters. The chapter closes with a look at one nonfinancial issue—sex education—and how it periodically gener-ated considerable controversy.

The Rise and Fall of Merit Pay

If employees are paid for performance in the private sector, why should a similar approach to compensation not work for public school teachers? Such reasoning apparently persuaded President Reagan to throw his support behind the drive to intro-duce merit pay in school systems. Even Virginia Democrats, including Governor Charles Robb, endorsed a form of merit pay for the purpose of rewarding talented teachers and increasing the likelihood that they would continue to teach. When a consulting firm was invited to study Fairfax's personnel policies in 1984, its recommendations reflected the times by calling for the develop-ment of an evaluation process that linked teacher pay to classroom performance. The School Board subsequently supported a limited test of the idea (Latimer, February 24, 1984). The pilot program originally designated participants as probationary, career, or master teachers based on their experience and performance. Master teachers would receive annual salary increases. Bonuses also would be used to recruit teachers for hard-to-fill positions and attract skilled teachers to troubled schools.

Local teacher organizations opposed the plan from the outset. Among their concerns was the possibility of arbitrary judgments by evaluators and questionable evaluation procedures. At the time, tenured teachers in Fairfax were observed several times every other year and given a rating of satisfactory, needs improve-ment, or unsatisfactory on various teaching functions. Administrators, however, did not always agree among themselves about what constituted acceptable and unacceptable performance, thereby buttressing teachers' apprehensions regarding merit pay. Superintendent Burkholder also wondered whether the school system could afford the $331,000 price tag for the pilot program (Latimer, May 19, 1984). Despite these objections, the School Board insisted on moving ahead with merit pay. When they

---

KEY DATES FOR FAIRFAX COUNTY PUBLIC SCHOOLS: 1984-2003

1984   School Board approves merit pay pilot program

1985   Robert R. Spillane appointed Superintendent

1987   FCPS begins to implement the Teacher Performance Evaluation Program

1988   Fairfax taxpayers approve $178.9 million bond issue for school construction

Virginia General Assembly mandates family life education in all school systems

1989   School Board refuses to support salary increases called for in original merit pay plan

School Board approves new family life education curriculum

1991   For the first time in decades, the School Board approves a budget lower than the previous year's budget

1993   Budget problems compel the School Board to phase out the merit pay plan

1995   Fairfax County holds School Board elections for the first time

1997   Daniel Domenech appointed Superintendent

2003   Consultant's report urges greater efficiency in delivery of special education services

---

replaced Burkholder in 1985, they specifically looked for a leader who could implement a merit pay plan.

An in-house assessment of the merit pay pilot following its first year revealed a variety of problems (Cohn, June 28, 1985). Faulting hasty planning, the report noted "confusion, inconsistency, miscommunication and frustration" regarding merit pay. School Board members were asked to support a cessation of the pilot, while a task force was convened to iron out the kinks. This delay also would give newly selected Superintendent Bud Spillane a chance to weigh in on the best way to proceed.

Spillane's first School Board meeting took place on July 11, 1985 (Cohn, July 12, 1985). The meeting was marked by two events that served to signify the increasing politicization of educational decision making in Fairfax County. First, Fairfax teachers demanded a role in designing any merit pay plan for the school system. Second, the School Board split along party lines in choosing a new vice-chairperson. At the time, Republicans controlled the county Board of Supervisors, and the Board of Supervisors chose members of the School Board. The School Board consisted of six Republicans and four Democrats. The headline in *The Washington Post* indicated that the party-line vote for vice-chairperson was a rarity for Fairfax County's School Board. What might have been an unusual occurrence in 1985, however, would come to typify School Board decision making in the years to follow.

For almost a year a group of Fairfax administrators, teachers, and community members debated the advantages and disadvantages of various approaches to merit pay. By September of 1986, a plan had been hammered out that both Spillane and leaders of Fairfax's largest teachers union, the Fairfax Education Association (FEA), could support. The plan, which came to be known as the Teacher Performance Evaluation Program (TPEP), entailed five components (Jones and Bohen, 1990):

1. professional growth opportunities for all teachers

2. recognition of and rewards for outstanding teaching performance

3. special assistance for teachers rated "marginal"

4. identification of teachers who failed to meet School Board mandated standards

5. systematic training for evaluators, teachers, and observers

When teachers were evaluated under the new plan, they received one of five ratings: exemplary, skillful, effective, marginal, and ineffective. These ratings became the basis for determining whether teachers could advance on Fairfax's "career ladder." The "career ladder" involved three steps—entry level, Career Level I, and Career Level II. Entry-level teachers had 3 years to meet standards and be placed on continuing contract status. Entry-level teachers who earned ratings of effective, skillful, or exemplary proceeded to Career Level I. Teachers with 7 years of experience in FCPS were eligible to seek Career Level II status. To qualify for Career Level II, a teacher had to be observed on multiple occasions and evaluated by a three-member team consisting of an administrator, a curriculum specialist, and a peer observer. Being designated a Career Level II teacher meant additional pay, greater professional responsibility, and release from annual performance-based evaluation. Career Level II teachers were evaluated every four years. In the interim they worked on customized professional growth plans.

In order to secure FEA support for the new evaluation process, Spillane had to back an ambitious salary improvement package that called for a 12.1 percent pay raise in the first year and two subsequent years of 8.8 percent increases. The initial price tag for implementing the pay-for-performance plan came to a hefty $97.5 million. This figure caused the original promoters of merit pay—county Supervisors and School Board members—to hesitate, however (Cohn, September 1, 1986). Fairfax principals also balked, expressing concern over having to evaluate teachers more frequently.

Because it was the first large school system in the United States to explore merit pay, Fairfax attracted considerable attention. National columnist William Raspberry (September 10, 1986) wrote that Fairfax's plan had "a lot going for it, not least of things the establishment of a career ladder that permits outstanding teachers to rise to better-paid, more prestigious positions on the basis of demonstrated skill, not just longevity and the accumulation of university credits." Raspberry went on to point out, however, that any merit pay plan was likely to "trigger charges of politics and favoritism" and "set teachers against each other." U.S. Secretary of Education William J. Bennett expressed unqualified support for the Fairfax plan, while using the occasion to denounce national education groups that opposed efforts to link teacher pay to performance (Cohn, November 22, 1986). For Fairfax school officials, though, what mattered most was what local taxpayers, not national observers, thought about the huge investment needed to launch merit pay.

Anticipating taxpayer resistance, the FEA announced that it would not support a rigorous new evaluation system for teachers without the salary improvement package. The FEA's rival, the Fairfax Federation of Teachers (FFT) refused to support the merit pay plan (Nelson, May 12, 1987). The FFT President, Rick Nelson, pointed out that teachers in the eight schools that had piloted the original merit pay plan raised a variety of objections, including poorly trained evaluators with limited teaching experience and highly subjective judgments of teacher performance. Of the 339 teachers evaluated during the pilot year, only 40 percent had earned ratings high enough to qualify for merit pay (Cohn, May 15, 1987). Teachers were not alone in their concerns about merit pay. Some School Board members feared that planners had failed to calculate the long-term financial impact of the pay raise package, especially with regard to the teachers' retirement plan. Teacher aides and clerical workers joined the chorus of complaint, noting that they also deserved salary hikes.

Fairfax's new Superintendent clearly had stuck his neck out politically by strongly backing the pay-for-performance plan. In order to cover the huge cost of implementing the TPEP, he had to declare a moratorium on all new educational programs, a decision that did not sit well with many constituents (Cohn, October 22, 1986). If he could not convince the School Board and the Board of Supervisors to fund the plan, Spillane's ability to lead the school system would be seriously compromised.

When the School Board voted on May 14, 1987, to adopt the pay-for-performance plan, no one was more relieved than Bud Spillane. TPEP was touted publicly as a way to make teacher evaluations more rigorous and weed out incompetent teachers. The new evaluation process would be phased in over a 2 year period. To earn a merit raise, a teacher would need to earn a top rating in each of eight performance categories. The categories ranged from knowledge of the curriculum to use of resources.

The adopted merit pay plan clearly was the product of compromise. All sides felt that they had made concessions. School Board chair Mary Collier, for example, had wanted to link student achievement to teacher evaluations, but she was forced to back down when the Fairfax Teachers Association registered strong opposition (Cohn, October 24, 1986). Fairfax school administrators successfully resisted the recommendation that every teacher be evaluated every year. When community members on the steering committee charged with planning the merit pay scheme complained that their suggestions were being ignored, the School Board added 11 community members to the committee (Cohn, May 15, 1987). Two months after giving their approval to a merit pay plan limited to classroom teachers, School Board members reversed themselves and voted to include librarians and counselors in the scheme. Later in July the Superintendent named three educators to join four FEA appointees on a review panel to address appeals by teachers who were denied merit increases. The FEA had lobbied strongly for such an appeals process.

When Fairfax teachers returned from summer vacation in 1987, Bud Spillane tried to allay their apprehensions regarding the new merit pay plan. He dispelled rumors that quotas had been set for the number of teachers who could apply for and receive bonuses (Cohn, September 1, 1987). Teachers were reminded, at the same time, that a 30 percent pay raise over three years demanded a rigorous accountability system. Two out of every five Fairfax teachers were scheduled to participate in the merit pay program during the 1987-1988 school year, with the remaining eligible teachers coming on board the following year.

Nine months later, as the first year of merit pay implementation drew to a close, the program's impact was debated throughout Fairfax County. Mimi Dash, president of the FEA, claimed that teacher morale had deteriorated at many schools, and over 100 grievances concerning job ratings had been filed (Cohn, May 31, 1988). School administrators complained that they were struggling to handle all of the extra teacher observations and evaluations. The Fairfax Federation of Teachers, which had opposed merit pay from the outset, picked up 270 disgruntled teachers who previously had been members of the FEA (Cohn, May 31, 1988). The School Board opted to slow down the implementation process so that concerns could be addressed.

When school officials released data on the first year of the new evaluation system, Fairfax residents learned that slightly more than 20 percent of the 3,400 participating teachers qualified for Career Level II. Only 135 teachers, or roughly 4 percent, were rated as "marginal" or "ineffective" (Cohn, May 31, 1988). School Board members were quick to add that an additional 150 teachers had quit or taken early retirement at midyear, when their preliminary ratings were received.

Cost estimates for converting to merit pay continued to be revised. By the spring of 1988, the original price tag of $97.5 million had been raised to $118.5 million. An additional $1.5 million was needed just to hire substitutes and teacher observers, so that evaluation data could be gathered. The long-term impact on pension benefits remained to be determined. Concerns related to fully funding the merit pay plan led to strained relations between the School Board and the Board of Supervisors.

Throughout the difficult days of implementation, Spillane continued to cheerlead for merit pay. When specific problems were detected in the plan, he supported reasonable adjustments, including the addition of monthly meetings between school administrators and FEA representatives in order to iron out wrinkles in the evaluation process (Travers, August 30, 1988). The Superintendent got a much needed vote of confidence in the fall of 1988, when 88 percent of FEA members expressed their support for his efforts to improve the new evaluation system (Heath, September 30, 1988). More good news came in October when a substantial drop in teacher absenteeism was attributed to merit pay (Baker, October 24, 1988).

Despite these encouraging signs, Fairfax officials realized that the fate of merit pay ultimately resided beyond their control. On August 1, 1988, the Board of Supervisors imposed a 10 percent ceiling on the increase in money the county would provide the school system for the coming school year (Baker, November 7, 1988). The Supervisors were described as "irritated" by "out-of-control school spending" and worried about growing taxpayer anxiety. The combination of fewer than expected dollars from the county and dwindling state funds spelled major problems for the teachers' new salary arrangement. To make matters worse, Fairfax taxpayers had just approved the largest bond issue in county history—$178.9 million—to fund school construction and renovation. School system planners warned that an additional $241.2 million would be needed to keep pace with county growth and capital improvement needs. Many wondered whether the welfare of Fairfax teachers would take a back seat to facilities demands. Representatives of the FEA reminded the community that they had been promised 30 percent raises over three years. The third year of the package was coming up. Spillane and the School Board countered that the best they could do for 1989-1990 might be bonuses instead of salary increases. Noting that bonuses deprived teachers of the pension benefits of salary increases, the FEA threatened to withdraw its support for the new evaluation system.

Fairfax teachers were pleased to discover that Spillane had taken their concerns to heart when he vowed to honor the original merit pay agreement. Despite a tight budget, the Superintendent went on record in late November as supporting raises for teachers earning the highest performance ratings (Baker, November 23, 1988). Backing up his verbal commitment, Spillane tabled $22.2 million worth of new projects in order to fund 10 percent merit raises (Baker, January 19, 1989). His decision brought immediate criticism from several Supervisors and School Board members who preferred to reduce the merit increases and fund the projects, which included class size reduction in low-achieving schools and equipment replacement. The majority of the School Board, however, backed the Superintendent. Or so he thought.

On February 14, 1989, Spillane and Fairfax teachers received an unwelcome Valentine from the School Board. Instead of the promised 10 percent raises for top-ranked teachers, the School Board voted in favor of 9 percent bonuses (Baker, February 15, 1989). The immediate consequence would be one-time awards of $2,600 to $3,900 for the Fairfax teachers—roughly one out of every four—who qualified for the top two ratings on the five-tiered scale. The head of the FEA, Walter Mika, pronounced the new evaluation system "dead" and characterized the School Board's decision as a "betrayal" (Baker, February 16, 1989). Spillane labeled the move a "compromise" and expressed the belief that "time will assuage some of that immediate anger." The fact remained, however, that the Superintendent had sustained his first major defeat in four years at the helm.

Merit pay was an idea closely tied to the Republican Party and President Ronald Reagan. Fairfax's willingness to step into the limelight with a pay-for-performance evaluation system had been a direct result of Republican control of the School Board. By 1989, however, Fairfax Democrats began to regain power. There were 5 Democrats on the 10-member School Board when the 1989-1990 budget for FCPS was approved, and 2 more Democrats were set to be appointed in the summer. It is fair to say that by 1989 the Democrats were less enamored of merit pay than their Republican counterparts. A *Washington Post* headline on March 9, 1989, predicted that a "rocky road" lay ahead for Fairfax's Superintendent and his pay-for-performance plan (Baker, March 9, 1989).

While some educational leaders might have read the political cards and accepted the inevitable, Bud Spillane was not about to back off his commitment to both rigorous teacher evaluation and merit pay. Vowing "no retreat," he circumvented union leaders and appealed directly to Fairfax teachers to make the new evaluation system work (Baker, March 17, 1989). Addressing teachers over the school system's cable television network, the Superintendent pledged to work through problems. FEA President Walter Mika stated that the union no longer supported the system and that teachers would not volunteer to undergo special evaluations in order to win bonuses. Spillane found himself at odds with FEA leadership as well as some School Board members.

Spillane counted on Fairfax teachers not wanting to jeopardize the monetary gains that had accompanied the new evaluation system. While the School Board might not have supported 10 percent salary increases for top-rated teachers, the fact remained that roughly one out of four Fairfax teachers had earned a 9 percent bonus. Ineffective teachers were being identified by evaluators and dismissed or compelled to resign. By the summer of 1989, Spillane could announce publicly that the merit pay system had been fully implemented and that it was "on target" in terms of its dual goals of rewarding talented teachers and removing incompetent teachers (Baker, July 20, 1989). Spillane received his own reward in July, when the School Board gave him a new 4-year contract. No sooner had the Superintendent embarked on his second term, however, than the newspapers announced that he was a finalist for the top post in the New York City school system (Baker, September 19, 1989). Many observers wondered whether the rancor over merit pay had prompted Spillane to consider moving on.

When Spillane was passed over in favor of Joseph Fernandez by the New York City Board of Education, speculation arose that his effectiveness in Fairfax might have been compromised by his willingness to entertain another superintendency. In the meantime, a new challenge to merit pay arose in the form of a class-action lawsuit (Baker, October 10, 1989). Seven African American teachers who did not receive merit bonuses sued the school system to nullify the merit pay program on the grounds that it discriminated against minorities. An analysis of the first two years of merit pay revealed that minority teachers indeed were less likely than white teachers to receive bonuses. A School Board member who had been in office at the time of the suit recalled that merit awards were much more likely to be earned by teachers at high-achieving schools. One way of interpreting this finding was that teachers blessed with bright students had more discretionary time to compile the portfolios and complete the paperwork required to qualify for Career Level II.

Another threat to Fairfax's Teacher Performance Evaluation Program was mounted in the spring of 1991, when the president of the FEA, Maureen Daniels, and the vice-chairman of the School Board, Laura McDowall, sought to scrap the system. An editorial in *The Washington Post* by Fairfax teacher Chuck Cascio (March 31, 1991) claimed that Daniels was motivated by concern that only a third of the FEA's membership qualified for merit bonuses, while McDowall sought to establish her credentials as a fiscal conservative in an effort to distance herself from the School Board chairman, a strong supporter of merit pay. The editorial took both to task, McDowall for allowing her desire for political influence to intrude on sound educational judgment and Daniels for reneging on union support for merit pay *after* Fairfax teachers had collected their hefty pay raises. The editorial wryly noted that the FEA made no offer to return the across-the-board salary hikes that had accompanied the new evaluation system.

McDowall (April 14, 1991) responded to Cascio's editorial by acknowledging her long-time opposition to merit pay, a position she argued was based on the fact that the pay-for-performance approach did not lead to improved teaching. McDowall also pointed out that the economic downturn of the early '90s could not be ignored. She implied that the $9.5 million spent on merit bonuses might be used more productively elsewhere.

A month after Cascio and McDowall squared off on the editorial page of *The Washington Post*, the Fairfax School Board sat down to finalize the 1991-1992 budget. For the first time in more than a quarter century, the budget would be less than the preceding year (Baker, May 24, 1991). Such drastic action had been necessitated by the Board of Supervisors' decision to reduce their allocation to the school system by $30 million. Sensing that the merit pay plan was in jeopardy, teachers who had been awarded merit bonuses spoke out publicly for the first time in support of the plan (Baker, May 23, 1991). Lined up against continuing merit pay in the face of serious economic conditions were both Fairfax teacher unions, several School Board members, and, in a reversal of its previous position, the Fairfax County Council of Parent-Teacher Associations. When the smoke of budget-cutting had cleared, merit pay remained. That the plan had defied odds-makers and survived was testimony to the collective voice of Fairfax's top teachers and effective behind-the-scenes maneuvering by the Superintendent.

While merit pay dodged a bullet in 1991, it eventually fell prey to continuing economic problems. With little left to cut, the financially strapped School Board started to phase out merit pay in 1993. The career ladder concept was abandoned, the evaluation cycle was lengthened from 3 to 5 years, and the last merit payment was scheduled for 1997 (Spage, Wang, and Chang, 2001).

Fairfax's brief experiment with merit pay and the Teacher Performance Evaluation Program illustrates many of the complexities of operating a large school system at the close of the 20th century. Innovations like merit pay and career ladders ultimately depend less on the educational value of the proposal than the political makeup of the School Board, the condition of the local economy, and the influence of teacher unions and other special interest groups. As the politicization of educational decision making in Fairfax intensified, the necessity of compromise increased. Bud Spillane proved to be unusually adept at preserving programs like merit pay through artful negotiation. In the end, however, even his leadership skills could not offset the impact of funding problems.

The Truest Test of Commitment

Educational policymakers take up considerable air time proclaiming their beliefs about a quality education, but the truest test of their commitment comes at budget time, especially when resources are scarce. To appreciate what Fairfax School Board members were willing to sacrifice and what they insisted on preserving, it is instructive to examine a year of financial crisis such as 1991. The previous section noted that merit pay barely escaped the budget ax that year. What programs were less fortunate, and what did efforts to cope with declining resources reveal about the values of the School Board and, ultimately, the community?

In the spring of 1991, as the United States struggled with a serious downturn in the economy, School Board members in Fairfax County prepared to slash $30 million from the 1991-1992 budget. Since a substantial part of the budget consisted of personnel costs, it was only natural that questions would be raised about the recent growth rate of the school system's workforce. *The Washington Post* reported on the eve of School Board budget deliberations that Fairfax's salaried employees had increased by 20 percent since 1985, compared to a 3.4 percent rise in student population (Baker, May 23, 1991). About 1,500 of the 2,500 new employees were teachers and teacher aides. Some observers began to ask whether Fairfax had been fiscally irresponsible in expanding its workforce so much during good economic times in the late '80s.

Sensing their vulnerability, Fairfax teachers tried to redirect the budget cutters. The president of the Fairfax County Federation of Teachers was quoted in *The Washington Post* as saying, "We've been telling the public for years now that if the School Board would cut unneeded bureaucracy, there would be more money for better instruction" (Baker, May 23, 1991). Spillane shot back, "If they [Fairfax teachers] want to make their own science kits, transport their own kids, do their own paperwork, bring in their own Xerox machines, then we'll get rid of" the additional support staff (Baker, May 23, 1991). Many of Fairfax's new positions could be traced to specific state or local initiatives, such as the requirement by Virginia that a guidance counselor be assigned to every elementary school and Fairfax's decision to shift high schools to a 7-period day. Hundreds of new ESL and special education teachers had been added in an effort to address Fairfax's increasingly diverse population. While the public generally understood the need for more teachers in specific areas mandated by law, they had more difficulty grasping a 35 percent increase in central office staff and a 50 percent jump in noneducational support staff, including computer operators, budget analysts, and engineers (Baker, May 23, 1991).

No aspect of Fairfax's educational program escaped the scrutiny of savings-hungry school officials. Even the extra funds for so-called special needs schools (schools with high percentages of low-achieving students), which many people believed were safe, wound up under the microscope. Special needs schools since 1984 had received extra staff positions and other resources in an effort to improve student performance. Roughly a quarter of Fairfax's 188 schools received special needs funding, which in 1990-1991 amounted to about $8 million (Baker, February 7, 1991). Forced to examine whether this extra money had made any difference, FCPS learned that test scores in special needs schools remained the same or declined. Few improvements had been made in dropout and retention rates. Spillane bit the bullet and informed the School Board that the time had come to reconsider the value of special needs funding. Robert E. Frye, the official minority representative on the Board and an early advocate for special needs funds, argued that the problem at hand was insufficient funding for schools with track records of low achievement. As he saw it, the school system had two choices, invest more money in the program or take existing special needs funds and concentrate them in a reduced number of schools. Since there was no extra money to invest, the choice, for Frye, was obvious.

On May 23, 1991, the School Board confronted the stark reality of the national recession and, following a directive from the Board of Supervisors, trimmed $30 million from Spillane's original budget. The approved budget amounted to $6.6 million less than the previous year's budget, the first decline in spending in more than a quarter century (Baker, May 24, 1991). To effect the

Education Empire

reduction, the School Board took a variety of steps, including freezing the salaries of all employees. This decision meant that 3.8 percent seniority raises would not be given. The president of the FEA protested that the School Board had violated its own policy mandating seniority raises. Fears were expressed that teacher pay in Fairfax, which averaged about $40,000, would fall behind neighboring divisions, thereby making it harder to recruit and retain talented teachers. Several board members also urged reducing the salaries of poorly rated teachers by 5 percent, but this measure was defeated by a 7-to-3 vote.

The School Board decided to eliminate 123 teaching positions, thereby increasing the student-teacher ratio by half a student. School officials maintained that the cuts could be made through attrition rather than firings. Other decisions included cutting the budget for athletic programs by 10 percent ($453,000), postponing the purchase of new language arts textbooks, and charging high school students $100 for parking privileges. Finally, the School Board directed the Superintendent to reduce his administration costs by $2.2 million. Having already eliminated 60 central office positions in March, Spillane now faced the prospect of axing 70 more.

In the aftermath of the May 23rd cuts, the Fairfax Education Association filed a lawsuit in Fairfax Circuit Court seeking to block FCPS from freezing teacher salaries (Baker, June 1, 1991). When this ploy failed, the FEA considered a "work-to-rule" action. School Board members defended their decision to freeze salaries as the only option besides making major cuts in classroom instruction.

As Fairfax employees struggled to cope with the effects, both material and psychological, of the 1991-1992 budget reductions, the Superintendent and his staff turned their attention to the 1992-1993 budget. On January 2, 1992, Spillane proposed increasing spending by 4 percent, despite county projections for an unprecedented revenue shortfall (Brown, January 3, 1992). His $903.2 million budget assumed a $38 million *increase* in county funding. The chair of the Board of Supervisors already had gone on record as saying the county would face a revenue shortage of $200 million. If the school system's programs had to be gutted, Spillane wanted to make certain that the Board of Supervisors bore the brunt of the blame. Such tactics consistently placed the Superintendent and the Supervisors at odds.

Spillane's proposed budget included cost-of-living raises for all employees, the restoration of seniority raises, and the retention of merit pay. It also called for continuing the 7-period school day for secondary schools—a $15.3 million item, reducing first-grade class sizes at certain elementary schools with large numbers of low-achieving students, and converting Baileys Elementary School to a magnet facility. To permit these costly measures, Spillane not only proposed raising the budget, he also recommended eliminating all student field trips and late buses for after-school activities and reducing summer school. A total of 833 jobs, including 327 teaching positions, would be eliminated as a result of the 1992-1993 budget. By sacrificing teaching positions to reinstate cost-of-living and seniority increases, Spillane tried to prevent an exodus of veteran teachers and win back the support of teacher leaders.

In the wake of the 1992-1993 budget proposal, public hearings produced predictable opposition to the threatened cuts (Brown, January 28, 1992). Maureen Daniels of the FEA urged the School Board to press for a tax hike, so that programs and jobs could be saved. Rick Nelson of the Fairfax County Federation of Teachers recommended eliminating merit pay and the 7-period day. When the Supervisors heard about Spillane's budget, they told the School Board to cut $26 million before officially presenting the budget to them in April. The Board of Supervisors was responsible for about three-quarters of the school system's revenues, but it lacked direct control over how education funds were allocated.

Under intense pressure to find ways to reduce the budget, the School Board announced its willingness to suspend merit pay, thereby saving $8.8 million annually (Brown, February 18, 1992). Spillane immediately challenged the decision, insisting that he would neither back down from a fight to preserve merit pay nor take the School Board's announcement as a signal for him to step down. Few observers, however, expected that the Superintendent would be able to resurrect merit pay. *The Washington Post* ran an article on the fate of merit pay plans across the nation (Brown, February 24, 1992). The article concluded that school systems were abandoning merit pay for individual teachers in favor of rewards for entire schools that succeeded in raising student achievement. Complaints that merit pay promoted divisiveness among teachers were cited as often as financial concerns as a justification for abandoning the incentive programs.

Dropping merit pay, of course, would account for only a portion of the budget reduction ordered by the Board of Supervisors. During the months before a final vote on the budget, Supervisors and School Board members argued about the best way to effect savings. School Board members preferred to cut positions and preserve cost-of-living increases, while supervisors insisted that salaries should be frozen for another year, so that class sizes would not have to be increased again. On May 29, 1992, the School Board voted to give teachers modest raises. According to many Fairfax educators, the process of trimming the 1992-1993 budget represented a low point in the history of the school system. Deputy Superintendent Jay Jacobs, a 27-year veteran of FCPS, resigned in dismay over the budget process, which he claimed pitted teachers against other school employees (Brown, June 3, 1992). Superintendent Spillane's future in Fairfax appeared to be in serious jeopardy (Brown, June 4, 1992). It was difficult to keep from wondering whether Fairfax County Public Schools could recover from the effects of two straight years of substantial budget reductions.

If there was a lesson to be learned from the haggling over how to cut the school system's budget, it was that the Superintendent, the School Board, and the Board of Supervisors could not be counted on to see eye-to-eye regarding what to cut. Each claimed to have the best interests of the school system and the community in mind, and each faulted the others for lacking insight into what was needed to sustain a great school system. Only a naïve observer would count on consensus in any future deliberations over the FCPS budget.

A New Millennium Brings Familiar Budget Woes

Fairfax County, along with the rest of the country, survived the economic downturn of the early '90s and rode out the rest of the century on an unprecedented wave of prosperity, fueled in part by the high-tech boom. Bud Spillane remained Superintendent until September of 1997, when the School Board elected not to renew his contract. Before he departed, he witnessed the first School Board election in Fairfax County. Virginia law had been changed in 1992 to permit localities to choose whether or not to elect School Boards. When the high-tech boom fizzled and the U.S. economy again lurched downward in 2001, Superintendent Dan Domenech would have to negotiate austerity budgets with an elected School Board. Was the process any different than it had been when Board members were appointed by county Supervisors?

In the spring of 2001, the Fairfax School Board consisted of seven Democrats and six Republicans. Teachers pressed for a cost-of-living increase, but in order to fund it the School Board needed to effect savings elsewhere. Republican Board members opposed raising class size by one student in order to meet teacher demands for a 3 percent increase. Six of the seven Democrats supported the increase as a necessary measure to keep teachers from exiting. One Democrat on the School Board, however, refused to support an increase in class size, thereby casting doubt that an across-the-board salary hike could be passed (Krughoff, May 9-15, 2001).

Increasing class size by one student would add $15.2 million to the general fund, enough to provide a 3 percent cost-of-living increase, but not enough to offset state and local revenue shortfalls. Coping with scarce resources is bad enough when enrollments are stable, but Fairfax's student population continued to grow, making the lack of funds even more serious. The budget submitted by Domenech proposed $12.5 million in cuts, including reductions for replacement equipment, maintenance, bus replacement, insurance liability, technology, and late bus runs. Instruction, too, was on the chopping block with cuts in the elementary gifted and talented program, field trips, focus and magnet schools, and the foreign language immersion program. Lest local residents think that these measures represented short-term stopgap cuts, the chair of the Board of Supervisors called the economic downturn facing northern Virginia and the nation "staggering" (Shear, April 24, 2001). And that was before the tragic events of September 11, 2001. One of those events, the crashing of an airliner into the Pentagon, took place on the very doorstep of Fairfax County and directly affected many of its citizens.

Despite mounting signs of a recession, Superintendent Domenech boldly proposed a $1.6 billion budget shortly after the beginning of 2002 (Seymour, January 4, 2002). The budget, which required a 12 percent hike in county support, included $136 million in new spending (a 9.2 percent increase over the previous school year). The lion's share of the new money was earmarked for growth in student enrollment (almost 3,000 new students), a 2 percent cost-of-living increase for all employees, and annual step increases for those who were eligible. Additional funds would be allocated to help students who failed Virginia's new Standards of Learning tests.

At the time that Domenech tendered his budget proposal, over 73 percent of FCPS's annual operating budget was funded by local revenue (MABE Guide FY 2002). This percentage had held remarkably steady since W. T. Woodson's era, when the local share of the school system's budget averaged between 66 and 70 percent (Walker, 1960). The remainder of the budget in 2001 was made up of state money (22 percent), federal funds (1.8 percent), and other resources including grants (2.3 percent). It is instructive to compare Fairfax with its fast-growing neighbor, Prince William County. Local taxes made up only 47.7 percent of Prince William's 2001 budget, with the state picking up 48.3 percent. No one could claim that Fairfax residents had failed to support their schools. There were limits, however, even for a relatively well-to-do county like Fairfax.

As the winter wore on, the likelihood of gaining approval for the ambitious budget diminished. Fairfax officials began to think tactically. In order to ~~~~~~~~~~~~~~~~~~~~~~~~~~~~~~~~~ on a new ~~~~~~ of allowing a developer to build the school and lease it back to the county (Seymour, February 22, 2002). Sensing that teacher raises were in jeopardy, division administrators searched for low-cost "perks" to mollify professional staff (Seymour, March 21, 2002). Proposals included increasing planning time for elementary teachers and ending the school year several days ahead of schedule by drawing on unused snow days. Besides searching for ways to save money, Fairfax leaders initiated a campaign to pressure state and federal authorities into allocating more money for education (Branigin, March 19, 2002). Domenech was especially critical of Virginia for failing to provide sufficient funds to permit local school systems to meet state mandates. In a letter to Fairfax employees, he noted that Virginia ranked 45th among the 50 states in state funding of local education (Supergram, February 13, 2002). The Superintendent estimated that Virginia needed to provide an additional $88 million if it expected FCPS to meet state curriculum mandates (Branigin, March 19, 2002). Furthermore, he pointed out that the federal government was short-changing the county by $50 million in impact aid. In years past, innovation in Fairfax meant coming up with new ways to address the educational needs of various groups of students. At the dawn of the new millennium, much of the creative thinking on the part of division leaders was redirected to coping with retrenchment.

April, the time when hearings on the county and school system budgets were scheduled, found antitax groups lobbying heavily for cuts in the tax rate (Rein, April 5, 2002). Several of Fairfax's neighbors already had reduced their tax rates. Realizing that such a decision in Fairfax could play havoc with the already endangered FCPS budget, Domenech issued a list of programs that would be at risk of being curtailed or eliminated if the Board of Supervisors lowered the property tax rate (Seymour, April 6, 2002). The list included many popular programs such as centers for gifted and talented third graders, foreign language immersion for first graders, and all fine arts and concert field trips. Class sizes also would have to be raised. Critics accused the Superintendent of resorting to an old ploy in order to scare taxpayers with children in school. Meanwhile Fairfax's county executive ordered his own department heads to find $50 million in savings in order to fund a reduction in the tax rate. If other county agencies, such as police and fire prevention, had to take a hit, taxpayers were likely to expect the school system to do the same.

By the end of April relations between the Supervisors and school officials were being characterized as a "feud" by *The Washington Post* (Rein, April 30, 2002). The Board of Supervisors went ahead and reduced the tax rate by 2 cents, but many citizens rallied around the school system. To mollify Fairfax parents, the Supervisors boosted school funding almost 9 percent by taking resources from other county agencies. Despite this gesture, Domenech argued that the school system remained $47 million short. His School Board backed him, expressing concern over the unwillingness of the Supervisors to tap their $75 million "rainy day" fund. The Supervisors responded that these funds were to be used only in case of an emergency. Clearly they did not regard the Superintendent's list of threatened programs and class size increases as an emergency.

Domenech refused to let the Supervisors off the hook. In early May he contended that Fairfax's neediest students were likely to suffer the most from proposed budget cuts (Seymour, May 10, 2002). The hit-list by this time had been expanded to encompass remedial assistance for students who did poorly on state Standards of Learning tests, several popular programs for low-achieving students, and school system payment for Advanced Placement and International Baccalaureate tests. The Superintendent indicated that such reductions could lead to a districtwide decline in test scores.

The budget finally approved in late May by the School Board represented a $90 million increase, from $1.08 billion in 2001-2002 to $1.17 billion in 2002-2003 (Branigin and Seymour, May 25, 2002). Board members despaired, however, that this increase would not offset the loss of $46 million in state aid and the increase in enrollment by 3,000 students. Some cuts were likely to have a much greater impact than others. Besides eliminating boys' varsity gymnastics, halving the schools' planetarium program, and postponing the purchase of new textbooks, the final budget increased class size, eliminated 80 jobs, curtailed the expansion of the Project Excel program for low-performing elementary schools, and reduced staffing for partial-immersion foreign language programs. The worst part of the budget process, though, were the warnings about what loomed ahead. Analysts estimated that Fairfax County Public Schools could face a funding shortfall of $60 million in 2003-2004. Even the finest school system cannot sustain year after year of bloodletting without eventually becoming anemic.

The School Board hired a consulting firm in 2003 to evaluate the efficiency and effectiveness of Fairfax's special education program. The consultant's report, presented to the Board in July of 2003, zeroed in on the high cost of educating students with special needs (Kalita, July 9, 2003). Operating special education centers resulted in annual costs ranging from $12,700 to $38,700 per special education student—82 percent more than the cost of educating a general education student. The report recommended closing two special education centers every other year, until the total had dropped from 21 to 5 or 6 centers. Too many Fairfax students, the report concluded, were being identified as eligible for special education services. Just over 14 percent of Fairfax students were involved in special education in 2003, but taking care of them required 22.6 percent of the school system's employees. The consultant's report was significant for several reasons. First, by going outside for an audit, the School Board showed that it was unwilling to rely exclusively on in-house program assessments. Second, by targeting a "sacred cow" like special education, the School Board demonstrated its commitment to leave no stone unturned in its search for savings.

Not everyone was pleased with the recommendations in the consultant's report. The Office of Special Education noted that the number of students assigned to special education centers already had been reduced from 7.5 percent to 5.2 percent of the special education population (Lewis and Mannie, 2003). Special education administrators insisted that many students with emotional disabilities needed the more restricted environment found in special education centers. They predicted that suspensions and expulsions would increase if these students were compelled to enroll in regular education classes. The quest for savings, however, prompted the School Board to consider options for reasons other than instructional impact.

Fairfax educators, despite their efforts to economize, had ample reason to feel anxious about the future as the November 2003 elections for the Board of Supervisors approached. Well before the elections, battle lines had been drawn between Fairfax Republicans, who insisted that local residents desperately needed property tax relief, and Fairfax Democrats, who worried that retaining the county's talented teaching force would be difficult if teachers received no salary increase. Democrats also expressed concern that two years of belt-tightening had eroded the school system's efforts to address the needs of at-risk students, non-English-speaking students, and gifted students. If the Republicans gained control of the Board of Supervisors, a property tax limitation similar to California's Proposition 13 was a distinct possibility. The predicted impact of such a measure on the school system was considered by many observers to be catastrophic.

The Politics of Sex Education

The preceding discussion may have left the impression that the only issues on which politics intruded on education were financial in nature. While the allocation of educational resources was the focus of considerable contentiousness in Fairfax County, other matters also provoked intense politicking. At various times during the '80s and '90s, for instance, School Board members battled over how reading and mathematics should be taught, whether teen mothers should be allowed to bring their babies to school, what services should be provided to homeschoolers, and the school system's position on charter schools. The teaching of creationism became a hotly debated issue in Fairfax's first School Board election in November of 1995 (O'Harrow, October 21, 1995). At least 12 of the 35 candidates in the inaugural election supported the teaching of "the history of creationism."

While the election was officially nonpartisan, both the Republican and the Democratic Parties, along with various special interest groups, endorsed candidates. The election resulted in victories for eight candidates endorsed by the Democratic Party and four candidates endorsed by the Republican Party. The success of the

Democratic candidates was attributed in part to a backlash against conservative candidates who had supported the teaching of creationism (Gamble, November 15, 1995).

One nonfinancial issue around which controversy has swirled, both before and after the advent of elected School Boards, is sex education. In March of 1988, the Democrat-controlled Virginia General Assembly passed a bill requiring all school systems to offer family life programs. Classroom instruction on matters ranging from drug and alcohol abuse to sex education was required to commence by September of 1989. Mary Ann Lecos, Assistant Superintendent for Instructional Services, indicated that Fairfax teachers already were covering about "90 percent of the state-mandated instruction." All that needed to be added was content regarding AIDS and family relationships ("Fairfax to Act on Sex Education," July 13, 1988). In a nod to local conservatives, Lecos chose as the head of the committee charged with planning the family life curriculum an individual who believed strongly in the value of teaching abstinence and involving parents in curriculum development.

As the committee completed its work in the spring of 1989, the school system faced a challenge to its own AIDS policy. A Fairfax parent whose daughter had the disease sued FCPS over its requirement that all parents in a school where a child with AIDS would be in attendance receive notification. The 4th U.S. Circuit Court of Appeals upheld the policy, noting that it "was reasonably structured so as to be unlikely to lead to identification of a particular student" ("Fairfax Schools' AIDS Policy Upheld," May 26, 1989).

When the proposed family life curriculum was presented to the community in hearings during the spring, substantial opposition surfaced (Baker, June 21, 1989). In the face of complaints about specific curriculum items and the timing of instruction in certain subjects, the Spillane administration modified various recommendations in the committee's proposal. The committee, for example, had suggested introducing contraception in the 7th grade, rather than the 10th grade, where it was being covered at the time. A "minority report" from the committee supported keeping the topic as part of the 10th grade "human life" unit. In an effort to compromise, Fairfax staff recommended moving contraception to the 9th grade. Other disagreements and compromise proposals surfaced around the topics of abortion, masturbation, and homosexuality.

On June 22, 1989, the School Board voted 9-to-1 to accept most of the staff recommendations regarding the family life curriculum (Baker, June 23, 1989). Unwilling to accept the compromises contained in the staff report, opponents threatened to "get even" during the upcoming November election of Supervisors. Apparently the right of parents to withdraw their children from any sex education unit was insufficient to appease the individuals and groups aligned against sex education. The lone dissenting School Board member succeeded in getting approval for an amendment that banned family planning centers and abortion clinics from being listed by the school system as "community resources for students."

Any observer who expected the sex education storm to blow over once the new curriculum had been adopted did not understand Fairfax politics. The county was home to too many high-powered and politically savvy citizens who were accustomed to getting what they wanted. They knew how to organize, apply pressure, and work the system. Thus it was that the newly formed Fairfax Citizens Council (FCC) filed legal papers in Fairfax Circuit Court in July to block implementation of the family life curriculum (Baker, July 22, 1989). The group claimed that the School Board had failed to heed "the outpouring of opposition from parents who complained that the curriculum would teach too much, too soon." School system officials felt vindicated in November when a Circuit Court judge threw out the legal petition, maintaining that the School Board had acted in a "factual, not fanciful" manner (Baker, November 11, 1989).

In May of 1990, the School Board completed the process of revamping the family life curriculum by unanimously approving lesson plans for a new four-week family life unit for 9th graders and a revised human life unit for 10th graders. The 9th grade unit, for the first time in Fairfax, covered the topic of homosexuality (Baker, May 25, 1990). In the fall, Fairfax teachers began implementing the new curriculum.

Students of the political process acknowledge that no decision is ever final. So it was the case that the issue of sex education was revisited when the makeup of the School Board took a conservative turn in 1994. Citing pressure from concerned parents, Republican-endorsed School Board members, led by chairman Gary Jones, decided on several revisions in the family life curriculum (O'Harrow, July 15, 1994). A first-grade book on diverse families was replaced because it "glorified" divorce. The lesson on AIDS was augmented with the message that "abstinence is the only safe choice." Three videotapes dealing with homosexuality, teenage parenting, and birth control were rejected because they promoted a "favorable viewpoint" on these subjects. The Board also expressed its intention to conduct an evaluation of the teaching of homosexuality and contraception. In reaching their decisions, the majority of School Board members overrode the recommendations of school system administrators and a citizens committee that recently had reviewed the family life curriculum.

The next issue at which the School Board took aim was a student survey of various risky behaviors. Originally designed by the national Centers for Disease Control and Prevention, the survey sought information regarding sexual activity and drug and alcohol use. Superintendent Spillane expressed his own reservations about certain elements of the survey. He particularly objected to asking students as young as 12 years of age when they last had sex ("Fairfax County School Board to Reconsider Its Support for Survey on Sex and Drugs," November 30, 1994). Supporters of the survey believed the information would be valuable in determining what to target in the family life curriculum.

Alarmed at the direction being taken by the School Board and aware of the impending inaugural election of Fairfax School Board members in November, a group of county residents formed the Fairfax Alliance for Responsible Education in the spring of 1995 (Lipton, June 15, 1995). The Alliance planned to investigate candidates' backgrounds and closely monitor the election. A spokesperson for the group declared, "The school system must maintain its integrity by not advancing any one group's narrow religious or social agenda" (Lipton, June 15, 1995). Republicans countered with their own concerns, chiefly the fear that the education of Fairfax children was at risk of being controlled by the local teachers union and, indirectly, the National Education Association. As the campaigning heated up, the election came to be viewed as a contest between backers of a variety of conservative positions, including limited sex education, inculcation of "family values," and the teaching of creationism, and those who generally supported the direction taken by Fairfax educators. The election's outcome, as indicated earlier, seemed to reflect support for the school system. At least for the moment.

A flap arose in the fall of 1997 when Fairfax's Family Life Curriculum Advisory Committee, made up of parents, students, health officials, religious leaders, and educators, recommended by a vote of 22-to-2 showing a new videotape about boys' development to fifth grade girls (Benning, November 19, 1997). Earlier in the year, after a mother of a fifth grade girl complained, Superintendent Spillane had ordered that this video, along with one about girls' development, no longer be shown to the opposite sex. By the time the committee made its recommendation, Spillane was no longer at the helm. The School Board voted 11-to-1 to broadcast the more controversial of the two videotapes on one of the school system's cable television channels, so that Fairfax parents could view it for themselves (Benning, December 5, 1997).

In an increasingly rare display of agreement, the School Board decided on December 18, 1997, to allow fifth graders to see videos about the physical development of the opposite sex (Benning, December 19, 1997). If Patricia Hersch's vivid account of the coming of age of Fairfax adolescents—*A Tribe Apart*—was any indication, their active sex lives clearly merited the Board's decision. Regardless of what parents might hope, sex was very much on the minds of many young adolescents in Fairfax County. It is worth noting that the Board's approval of the videotapes was contingent on editing out details about male erection for fifth grade girls and information on menstruation and feminine hygiene for fifth grade boys.

A Balancing Act

Being an educator in an affluent suburban county with many highly educated and well-connected residents can be both a blessing and a curse. As long as resources are plentiful, residents of Fairfax County have been supportive of most efforts by their school system to create innovative programs and provide students with learning opportunities unavailable in less well-to-do districts. Over the years, Fairfax parents have come to rely on and expect high quality educational services.

The economic ups and downs of recent decades have taken their toll, however, on the relative harmony that once characterized educational decision making in Fairfax County. While it would be incorrect to pretend as if there were once a time when School Board members, Supervisors, parents, and school leaders saw eye to eye on every issue, a case can be made that individuals in the past were far more likely to set aside political affiliations and personal agendas for the common good than they are today. As Fairfax has become more diverse and growth has outstripped resources, various groups served or affected by the public schools have felt the need to organize and engage in special interest politics. The advent of elected School Boards has facilitated this trend, as Board members now must campaign for their seats. According to several Board members, campaigning has led would-be Board members to make promises designed to benefit their constituents. In the process, the interests of residents of particular magisterial districts have been pitted against those of their neighbors.

School systems in Virginia may be required by law to balance their budgets, but nowhere is it mandated that they must balance competing interests. Still, it is fair to argue that the effective operation of an education empire like Fairfax County Public Schools demands a careful and continuous balancing of competing interests. Balancing competing interests, of course, is easier said than done. Some groups' interests are protected by law. Others, such as students who are neither designated "disabled" nor "gifted," are not. At a given point in time, some groups invariably enjoy more political clout and access to resources than other groups.

Fairfax school leaders have learned that they must not only understand the political process, they themselves must become political actors. Faced with tight resources, they have gone on the offensive and lobbied Richmond and Washington for additional funds. They have campaigned locally for resources that otherwise might have been allocated to other public services. In the process, they have become especially adept at keeping competing interests in check. When high growth areas of the county have received new schools and services, school officials have assured residents of other areas that their children will not be shortchanged. When the needs of low-achieving students have been addressed, parents of gifted students have been guaranteed that honors programs will not be sacrificed. School system leaders even have made an effort to balance programmatic requirements against employees' needs for competitive salaries and good working conditions. If they have failed to satisfy everyone, it is not for lack of trying.

CHAPTER 5

· Good Isn't Good Enough

It is a difficult challenge to *maintain* existing levels of student achievement, when a school system is growing and resources are not keeping pace. It is an even taller order to *raise* student achievement during such circumstances. This, however, is precisely the challenge that Fairfax County Public Schools has faced since the mid-'90s. The bar initially was raised by the state of Virginia, when it adopted new curriculum standards and high-stakes tests aligned to the standards. Then the federal government followed suit with the No Child Left Behind Act. Chapter 5 takes a closer look at how Fairfax County Public Schools has responded to these initiatives.

Richmond Sends a Message

Irony is no stranger to politics. Still, Virginia educators could not help being puzzled when a Republican governor, George Allen—who had run on a campaign highly critical of the ever-expanding reach of state government under his Democratic predecessors, set into motion the most comprehensive educational accountability initiative in state history. The initiative had the effect of increasing state control over virtually every aspect of local education.[1]

First came a revised set of curriculum requirements, referred to as the Standards of Learning (SOL). Accusations of partisan politics accompanied the drafting of the SOL. The Allen administration had pledged to rely on input from professional educators in developing the curriculum standards, but no sooner were recommendations received from teacher groups in four school systems, including Fairfax County, than Governor Allen's handpicked Champion Schools Committee developed its own curriculum standards. On

119

KEY DATES FOR FAIRFAX COUNTY PUBLIC SCHOOLS:
1995-2003

1995   Virginia Board of Education approves Standards of Learning

1997   Virginia Board of Education approves Standards for Accrediting Public Schools

        Daniel Domenech appointed Superintendent

1998   Success by Eight program is launched

1999   43 out of 203 FCPS schools meet new accreditation standards, based on state tests

        Project Excel is initiated

2001   75% of FCPS schools meet state accreditation standards

        Fairfax voters approve $378 million bond issue for capital improvements

2002   U.S. Congress passes No Child Left Behind Act

2003   Virginia Board of Education adopts plan for complying with No Child Left Behind

---

June 22, 1995, the Virginia Board of Education approved the SOL for every grade in mathematics, science, and language arts. Action on social studies standards, the most controversial area of the K-12 curriculum, was postponed.

The next step in Virginia's accountability plan involved the development of standardized tests aligned to the SOL. The Virginia Department of Education contracted with Harcourt Brace to create and field test 27 tests. The plan called for students to be tested in English and reading, mathematics, science, and history at grades 3, 5, and 8. High school students would be tested at the completion of specific courses. Fifth and eighth graders also would be given a technology test. Graduation requirements were raised at this time, to 22 credits for a Standard Diploma and 24 credits for an Advanced Studies Diploma. Six of the 22 credits for a Standard Diploma and 9 of the 24 credits for an Advanced Studies Diploma had to be *verified* credits, meaning students had to earn a passing grade in a course *and* pass the state standardized test aligned to the course's content.

On September 4, 1997, the Virginia Board of Education adopted a new set of Standards for Accrediting Public Schools in Virginia. The accreditation standards generated considerable controversy. A group of northern Virginia lawmakers, in fact, tried to derail Governor Allen's initiative early in 1997. They feared that the accreditation standards reflected the antipublic-education views of political conservatives on the Virginia Board of Education (Hsu and O'Harrow, January 18, 1997). Richmond's agenda, they speculated, might be to "set up local schools to fail," thereby eroding support for public schools and paving the way for tuition vouchers for private schools.

The northern Virginia lawmakers were unsuccessful in their efforts, and the new Standards of Accreditation (SOA) went into effect in the fall. Among other provisions, the SOA required every public school to achieve minimum passing rates on SOL tests in order to be fully accredited. Passing rates were to be determined by political appointees on the state Board of Education, not by educators. Beginning in 2004, students who failed to earn sufficient verified credits would be denied a high school diploma. Schools that did not achieve specified passing rates on SOL tests would lose accreditation and be subject to sanctions beginning in the 2006-2007 school year. To ensure that every community was kept apprised of how its schools were doing, Virginia also mandated the annual publication of a School Performance Report Card for every public school. Parents and other community members could see at a glance the percentage of a school's students who had passed particular SOL tests and the school's accreditation status. A new era in Virginia education clearly had begun. How would Fairfax County contend with the demands of statewide accountability?

Fairfax Rises to the Challenge

The timing was not the best. Just as Fairfax confronted the new era of educational accountability, it had to replace Bud Spillane. The individual chosen by the School Board, like his predecessor, had extensive administrative experience in northern school systems. Both men had been finalists for New York City's top education post. Born in Cuba and fluent in Spanish, 52-year-old Dan Domenech had most recently served as a regional superintendent

on Long Island. No one needed to remind the new chief of the politi-
cized nature of educational decision making in Fairfax County.
Domenech's selection had been a split decision, with the Democratic
majority favoring his candidacy and the Republican minority backing the Superintendent of Madison, Wisconsin, schools.

Domenech wasted no time in making his agenda clear. The
headline announcing his selection in *The Washington Post* said it
all—"Good Isn't Good Enough for Fairfax School System"
(Mathews and Benning, November 16, 1997). The article noted
that School Board members had no intention of allowing the school
system to "coast" on its fine reputation. No longer would Fairfax's
success be measured against other school systems. Instead,
Fairfax would establish its own benchmarks for academic achievement. Systemwide goals were not long in coming. Declining to wait
until the results of Virginia's first round of SOL tests were in,
Domenech developed an ambitious set of goals to guide the division over the course of his first full year in office. They included
the following (Benning, September 3, 1998):

- All county schools will meet new state goals that call for 70
  percent of their students to pass new statewide tests in
  basic subjects.

- The percentage of students scoring above the national
  average on the Scholastic Aptitude Tests (SATs) will
  exceed last year's percentage, and the gap between SAT
  scores of minority and white students will narrow by 10
  percent.

- At least 25 percent of high school students will have
  enrolled in at least one Advanced Placement (AP) or
  International Baccalaureate (IB) course, and at least two-
  thirds of those students will score 3 or higher on the corresponding AP exam, or 4 or higher on the corresponding IB
  exam.

- The percentage of students who take and pass Algebra I
  before the ninth grade will be increased, and the gap
  between white and minority students taking the course
  will be narrowed by at least 25 percent.

- Overall suspension rates, and the disparity in the suspension rates for white and minority students, will be reduced
  by 10 percent.

- All schools will have at least 40 percent of the high-end computers that central staff proposed when setting school-by-school targets last year.

- At least 40 percent of all instructional and administrative personnel will meet or exceed Virginia technology competency standards.

- Schools will show at least a 25 percent reduction in the recidivism rate for students suspended because of acts of violence.

- The School Board will approve a more flexible staffing and funding approach to better address the needs of individual schools.

- A multiyear funding source to pay for long-range technology improvements will be identified, and an implementation plan will be developed.

Reviewing the school system's goals for 1998-1999, it is clear what the guiding concerns were. Ensuring that all schools met Virginia's new accreditation standards was job one. Raising overall achievement while narrowing the gap between white and minority performance did not surprise anyone familiar with Fairfax's priorities in recent years. Neither did remaining in the forefront of educational applications of computer technology, addressed in three separate goals. Many school system veterans breathed a sigh of relief when they saw the goal concerning flexible staffing and funding for individual schools. The new Superintendent apparently had no intention of trying to standardize the way that individual Fairfax schools met their achievement targets. The latitude accorded principals and their faculties to improve performance had become a hallmark of Fairfax County Public Schools since the '70s and was regarded by many local educators as a key to the school system's success.

One of the most publicized of Domenech's initiatives was the "Success by Eight" program, which aimed to have all students performing at grade level in basic skills, especially reading, by the time they entered the third grade. Set to be piloted at six elementary schools in 1998-1999, "Success by Eight" initially called for grouping students in kindergarten through second grade by skill level and interest rather than by grade and age. Each school day, students would be grouped and regrouped for different types of instruction. Instructional staff would not work in self-contained classrooms, but instead would be deployed in ways that allowed them to provide students with more individual attention. "Success by Eight" schools also included full-day kindergartens, rather than the half-day programs at other Fairfax elementary schools.

Based on the results of pilot tests in the six schools, "Success by Eight" was expanded the following year. Elementary schools that applied to participate in the program had to demonstrate how they would draw on "quality early childhood practices" to ensure that all students performed at grade level by the end of second grade. Practices endorsed by FCPS included flexible grouping, active and hands-on learning, differentiated instruction, learning stations, and "authentic assessment." Among the additional resources awarded to schools that successfully competed for "Success by Eight" status was funding for a full-day kindergarten program.

Other initiatives launched during the new Superintendent's first full school year in office included a year-round program at Timber Lane Elementary, two new International Baccalaureate programs at Edison High School and Robinson Secondary School, and two new high school academies—an international studies, business, engineering, and scientific technology academy at Edison and a communications arts academy at Fairfax High School. Both academies were open to students from across the county. Additional choices were offered in the form of 10 new focus elementary schools. Belle View and Hybla Valley's "focus" was the "core knowledge" curriculum made famous by the University of Virginia's E. D. Hirsch. Centreville, Forest Edge, Garfield, Greenbriar East, Greenbriar West, Gunston, Newington Forest, and Westlawn became "basic schools" with substantial community involvement in goal setting and a focus on language, mathematics, and the arts. At the middle-school level, two pilot programs were launched. Glasgow Middle School introduced intensive assistance for all students in reading and mathematics. Kilmer Middle School augmented its gifted and talented program, creating high-tech labs to enable students to conduct research projects and beefing up mathematics and science offerings. In a further move to promote academic improvement, the school system introduced a new requirement that all students taking Advanced Placement courses had to take the corresponding AP or IB examination. To appreciate the significance of this move, it is important to know that Domenech also insisted that enrollment in Advanced Placement and International Baccalaureate courses be open. In other words, any high school student who wished could select a rigorous course in either program. Requiring all students enrolled in AP and IB courses to take external exams meant that teachers of these courses were expected to teach *all* their students, not just a select few who would be encouraged to sit for exams. Reviewing this list of initiatives, it is clear that Dan Domenech and his administration had decided that FCPS would not rest on its laurels.

Fairfax County is not the kind of community where goals are set and then forgotten. The school system is blessed with the research and evaluation capacity to monitor progress on division goals, which is fortunate because School Board members and their constituents took a keen interest in how the school system was doing under its new leader. A year after Domenech's initial set of systemwide goals appeared in *The Washington Post,* a follow-up piece examined the extent to which the goals were being achieved ("School Goals: Hits and Misses," September 2, 1999). The most alarming finding was that only 43 of Fairfax's 203 schools met state accreditation standards on the second administration of the SOL tests. As far as the new state accountability program was concerned, Fairfax clearly had a lot of work to do.[2]

The progress report also contained a number of positive findings. The number of high school students taking Advanced Placement tests rose by 52 percent. The percentage of these students earning a score of 3 or better dropped, however, from 77 percent in 1997-1998 to 64 percent in 1998-1999. The percentage of both white and minority students taking Algebra I before the ninth grade increased. Suspension rates dropped, both for minority students and for students in general. Progress also was noted in equipping schools with high-end computers and training staff members in the use of technology.

To address the issue of inadequate performance on the new state tests, Domenech announced a pair of new initiatives aimed at academic improvement and accountability (Benning, September 2, 1999). The first called for every school in the system to have its own set of academic goals. The second effort, and the "centerpiece" of the Superintendent's assault on low performance, was Project Excel. Project Excel initially focused on the 20 elementary schools with the largest percentages of students at risk of failing the SOL tests. Each school was characterized by low standardized test scores, a high student mobility rate, high percentages of poor and minority families, and high numbers of non-English-speaking students. In keeping with Fairfax's tradition of flexible school funding, extra resources—$8 million in the first year—were funneled to Excel schools. The schools were required to choose one of several "curriculum models" with a proven track record, and each was permitted to operate a full-day kindergarten. Schools had 3 years to raise their passing rates on state tests. Domenech appointed a special task force to determine possible rewards and sanctions for Excel schools. Eventually it was decided to award every staff member in an Excel school a bonus of up to $2000, if the school achieved its performance targets. Fairfax was shifting its approach to accountability from one focused on each individual teacher's accomplishments to a collective accountability model based on an entire faculty's performance.

Evidence that Fairfax teachers and students had responded to the challenge of statewide "high stakes" testing was not long in coming. When the results of spring tests became available in September of 2000—3 years after the first tests were administered—dramatic improvements had been made (Benning, September 15, 2000). A total of 82 Fairfax elementary schools reached the critical benchmark of 70 percent passing rates, compared to only 7 schools in 1998. The number of middle schools and high schools achieving their benchmarks rose from 4 to 13 and 2 to 11, respectively. While there was good reason to celebrate, Domenech reminded Fairfax parents and staff members that there were still a substantial number of students who would not meet graduation requirements, if the state standards set to go into effect in 2004 were already in place. He also reiterated his belief that Virginia should not make the SOL tests the sole basis for determining which students would graduate and which schools would be accredited. This view was shared by a number of his constituents (Benning, September 28, 2000).

To track the progress of Project Excel schools, Fairfax evaluation specialists created the Schoolwide Achievement Index (SAI). The SAI was computed from students' scores on SOL tests in English, mathematics, science, and history, as well as the state-mandated Stanford 9 TA tests. According to one School Board member, a primary purpose of the SAI was to reveal whether students in a school's bottom quartile were making progress. Previously, these students' performance could be offset by the scores of high-achieving students, thereby creating the false impression of satisfactory schoolwide performance.

When the results of the 2000-2001 tests became available and SAIs were computed for the 20 Excel schools, 19 recorded increases over the previous year ("Celebrating Success," 2002). The Superintendent proudly announced that 13 of the 20 schools achieved "gold award" status by virtue of having met or exceeded all of their targets for improved test results. Overall, Excel schools' gains on SOL tests more than doubled those for the entire division, and almost tripled divisionwide gains in mathematics. Project Excel had demonstrated that focusing resources and expertise on needy schools could produce impressive results. Based on these successes, Domenech expressed his desire to add 8 more at-risk elementary schools to Project Excel in 2002-2003.

What specific interventions were credited with turning around the Excel schools? According to "Celebrating Success," a school system publication spotlighting the 13 gold award Excel schools, each school relied on (1) a research-based instructional model that was endorsed and implemented by faculty members, (2) increased time for learning (based on such adjustments as full-day kindergarten, extended school days, and a modified school calendar), (3) technology-based phonics instruction for grades K-1, (4) a school-wide focus on analyzing assessment data and determining the instructional needs of students, and (5) staff development targeted to identified student needs. Among the instructional models adopted by particular schools were Direct Instruction, Reading Recovery High Impact, and Success for All. In addition to importing proven programs, Excel schools developed their own interventions. Groveton Elementary, for example, promoted teacher collaboration by assigning special education and ESOL instructors to each grade-level team. Glen Forest Elementary relied on its business-school partnerships to provide students with mentors, tutors, and access to cultural activities. Annandale Elementary stressed the importance of reading and effective communications during an uninterrupted daily 2-hour language arts block. As in other Fairfax initiatives, Project Excel encouraged local variation within a common districtwide framework.

To provide middle and high school students with more time to prepare for state SOL tests in the spring, Stuart and Falls Church High Schools and Glasgow Middle School began the 2001-2002 school year 2 weeks early (Samuels, August 21, 2001). The modified calendar, which also was followed by five Fairfax elementary schools, reduced the length of the summer break. In order to switch to the new calendar, at least 60 percent of a school's parents had to give their approval. To boost scores on the SAT, Fairfax budgeted $120,000, so that every sophomore could take the PSAT and find out where they needed additional preparation.

Educators acknowledge that it typically is much more difficult to turn around a low-performing secondary school than it is to improve an elementary school. Fairfax officials therefore felt doubly proud when Stuart High School was spotlighted in *Education Week* (Bartlett, August 6, 2003). The article characterized Stuart as "an embodiment of polyglot America in the 21st century." The school's enrollment of 1,450 students consisted of Hispanics (30%), whites (27%), Asians (20%), Middle Easterners (12%), and blacks (11%). Fifty-four percent of Stuart's students qualified for free or reduced-price lunch, and 7 out of 10 were born outside the United States. The mobility rate was 30 percent.

In 1998 Stuart students' performance on Virginia's SOL tests placed them last among Fairfax's 21 high schools. Five years later Stuart ranked ahead of 8 Fairfax high schools, including schools serving far more affluent families. Nine out of 10 Stuart students graduated from high school, and in 2002 an impressive 99 percent of those graduates went on to 2- or 4-year colleges. According to Cluster Director John English, Stuart students are performing two standard deviations above their predicted achievement, based on the school's poverty level. Forty percent of Stuart students are enrolled in International Baccalaureate courses, and 8 out of 10 of these students get at least a 4 on the IB exam. The figure for the entire school system is 67 percent. The Bill and Melinda Gates Foundation chose Stuart High School and its feeder schools as 1 of only 10 recipients of its prestigious High Risk/ High Reward Award.

What factors have accounted for this success story? Buzz Bartlett, the president of the Council for Basic Education and author of the piece in *Education Week*, pinpointed several contributing factors. Foremost on his list was the leadership of principal Mel Riddile, who devised various ways of promoting a culture of continuous improvement at Stuart. Besides keeping the focus of faculty attention on student achievement data, he initiated an automated phone service that contacted perennial oversleepers and reminded them to come to school. Such efforts raised Stuart's attendance rate from 89 percent in 1997 to 96 percent in 2003. Riddile also relied heavily on the leadership of his department chairs and on cohesive faculty teams that shared responsibility for addressing specific performance problems.

John English added several other factors that helped explain Stuart's impressive turnaround. The previously mentioned modified calendar that required students to start school early in August enabled them to get almost a month more preparation for the spring SOL tests than their counterparts in other Fairfax high schools. Stuart also operated 2 summer sessions for students at risk of failing state tests. Funding from the Excel program allowed Riddile to reduce class sizes to some of the lowest in the school system. Algebra and Transitional English, two linchpin courses for academic success, were double blocked, so that low-achieving students could receive twice as much exposure to course content. A crucial factor, in English's opinion, was Stuart's heavy emphasis on reading. Besides annually assessing all students on reading, the high school boasted a "reading across the curriculum" initiative that considered *all* teachers to be reading teachers. The last element in Stuart's efforts to boost achievement involved technology. As a result of the school system's commitment to support the high school, Stuart went from having 1 computer for every 8 students in 1997 to 1 computer for every 1.8 students in 2003.

More Signs of Success

While Stuart High School's success story is impressive, it is by no means the only Fairfax school to register significant gains in student achievement. When the results of spring 2001 state tests were received the following September, Fairfax educators were gratified to see that their efforts to boost student performance were making a difference (Seymour, September 7, 2001). The number of schools meeting benchmarks for state accreditation jumped to 75 percent from 63 percent the previous year. Only 5 percent of Fairfax schools received an "accredited with warning" designation. Writing was a particular bright spot, with 92 percent of Fairfax fifth graders passing the state test. The track record for schools involved in the division's various special initiatives was especially laudable. Of the 20 Excel schools, 17 improved on the state SOL tests. Nine of the 14 Success by Eight schools gained on the SOL tests, and 4 of the 5 year-round schools made substantial gains (Seymour, November 26, 2001).

Asked to account for Fairfax's outstanding results, Domenech indicated that there was no magic involved, just continual staff development, an unwavering focus on the curriculum, and unrelenting assistance for students who needed help. While he was at it, the superintendent might also have reminded people of the role of extra resources for low-performing schools. Additional funding for special needs schools had yielded such remarkable results, in fact, that Domenech expressed the desire to expand such programs to include 16 other schools with large numbers of poor and immigrant families (Seymour, November 26, 2001). The estimated cost to create eight more Excel schools, six additional Success by Eight schools, and two more year-round schools was $7.5 million.

Fairfax educators had little time to exult over the news of student achievement gains. Four days after the initial report in *The Washington Post*, the tragic events of September 11, 2001, reminded people that there were more important matters than scores on standardized tests. Fairfax schools closed in the immediate aftermath of the terrorist attacks, as school officials reviewed crisis management and school security plans. It would not be the last time that the entire school system had to face a serious threat to the safety of students and employees. A year after 9-11, schools in northern Virginia were confronted by the sniper shootings, resulting in the canceling of outside activities and the relocation of athletic contests.

In the fall of 2001, state test results also took a backseat to the biggest school bond issue in Virginia history. Fairfax taxpayers were asked to support a $378 million bond earmarked for renovating and replacing outdated school facilities. The timing was not opportune, given the freefall of the post 9-11 economy. Considering growing concerns about local, state, and national revenues, it was not surprising that questions began to surface regarding the substantial amounts of money the school system was spending on special initiatives. Domenech's $25 million-a-year effort to raise the achievement of non-English-speaking-students, for example, caused at least one Supervisor to ask for evidence that the money was being well spent (Seymour, October 1, 2001). Some observers questioned the trade-offs involved in providing extra funds to special needs schools. The implication was that, in order to reduce class sizes in these schools, class sizes elsewhere had to be increased.

True to his humble origins, Domenech remained steadfast in his commitment to providing as much assistance as possible to Fairfax's neediest students. He was quoted in *The Washington Post* as follows:

> I like to use the analogy of a race. The frontrunners, those are the kids who are never gonna run behind. But the kid who doesn't speak English, the child who is never read to

at home, who has never gone to the zoo, who has never been on a plane—there's a catch-up. We need to give them above and beyond what we give the other kids. (Seymour, October 1, 2001)

On November 6, 2001, Virginians went to the polls and elected Mark Warner, the first Democratic governor in 8 years. Of more immediate importance to Fairfax County Public Schools, local voters, by a 4 to 1 ratio, passed the $378 million bond issue. The enormous sum would enable the school system to build or renovate 30 elementary, 2 middle, and 10 secondary or high schools. Domenech regarded the margin of victory as a mandate for the division's educational policies as well as its facilities needs. He even suggested that the vote implied that northern Virginians were prepared to raise the local sales tax in order to improve education funding (Seymour, November 7, 2001). The superintendent did not bank on continued economic stagnation. When the School Board finally approved the budget for 2002-2003, the Superintendent's plans for expanding proven programs for the school system's neediest students had to be curtailed. Even demonstrated success could not guarantee that adequate funds would be available for school improvement.

No Child Left Behind

No sooner had Fairfax made the necessary adjustments to meet the demands of Virginia's comprehensive accountability plan than the administration of George W. Bush launched a national educational accountability initiative. Signed into law on January 8, 2002, the No Child Left Behind Act (NCLB) affected every school system that received federal Title I assistance. At the state level, NCLB called for the establishment of performance standards for all schools and the identification of Title I schools that failed for two consecutive years to make adequate yearly progress toward meeting the standards. The determination of what constituted "adequate yearly progress" was left up to the individual states. Schools found to be deficient were required to develop improvement plans. The process of developing these plans needed to involve parents, school and district staff, and outside experts. NCLB even suggested the kinds of improvement interventions schools should consider (Brady, 2003). One of the most controversial provisions of the act required school systems to offer students enrolled in failing or unsafe schools the option to transfer to other public schools in the district, including charter schools.

NCLB went further to consider what to do with failing schools that were unable to improve despite implementing a corrective plan. First, students in these schools must have access to extra tutoring from parent-selected and state-approved providers. After 2 years of inadequate progress, schools on improvement plans are subject to "corrective action," including replacement of staff, extended learning time for students, and school restructuring. Continued failure to make adequate progress leads to more drastic measures, such as reopening the school as a charter school and outsourcing school operations to an external provider.

Largely because Virginia's accountability plan was so comprehensive, Fairfax County Public Schools already had initiated a number of policies, programs, and practices that addressed the intent of NCLB. Projects like Excel and Success by Eight constituted excellent examples of school improvement efforts that worked. In some cases, though, the new federal legislation still presented FCPS with unanticipated challenges.

On January 28, 2003, the Virginia Board of Education adopted a plan for complying with the No Child Left Behind Act. The state bar was set high, even for a school system as successful as Fairfax County Public Schools. By 2013-14, the Board's plan required that *every* student pass SOL tests. Benchmarks also were set for pass rates on tests in the years leading up to 2013-14. In 2003-2004, for example, 61 percent of a school's students had to pass the SOL reading tests and 59 percent the SOL mathematics tests. These percentages also were required for subgroups of students, including students from different minority groups, special education students, and students who qualified for free or reduced-price lunch.

Language-minority students were not excluded from the regulations. Prior to NCLB, these students could be exempted from tests for 5 years, so that schools could prepare them properly. The new law reduced the preparation time to 3 years. In addition, all parents of children receiving special instruction in English, beginning at kindergarten, had to be notified that extra help was being provided. Because FCPS allowed language-minority students to be exempt from tests for only one year, NCLB created fewer shockwaves in Fairfax than elsewhere.

School systems as well as schools are held accountable under NCLB. As students returned to school in September of 2003,

Virginians learned that few school systems in the state had made sufficient progress on SOL tests to meet the requirements of NCLB (Helderman, September 12, 2003). Fairfax fell short of the mark because some special education students had not taken SOL tests in reading and mathematics. Plans were made, according to Ray Diroll, the head of FCPS's Office of Student Testing, to test these students in 2003-2004, thereby bringing the school system into full compliance.

The paperwork requirements associated with NCLB posed enormous problems for school systems as large as FCPS. To determine whether all teachers were qualified to teach their assignments, the law mandated background checks on college majors and teaching credentials for every teacher. Furthermore, NCLB also specified that all teaching assistants needed to have at least an associate's degree or a passing grade on a state certification test. With over 1,800 teacher aides and a pre-NCLB requirement of only a high school diploma, Fairfax faced a time-consuming and costly job of catching up.

Before he departed for a superintendency in Illinois, Deputy Superintendent Alan Leis pointed out several additional challenges presented by NCLB. First, the law was based on the goal of continuous improvement. Schools that did not demonstrate continuous improvement were subject to sanction. Leis observed that it is one thing for a low-achieving school to keep boosting performance and quite another matter for a school that already is achieving at or near the top. Fairfax was blessed with a large number of high-achieving schools. With little room left for improvement in these schools, what had been a blessing could become a curse under the new legislation.

A second problem identified by Leis concerned the enormous task of recordkeeping required for a data-driven accountability system. Both NCLB and the Virginia accountability plan called for continuous monitoring of individual students' achievement. Designing an information management system is difficult enough for a school system with a stable student population. When a high level of student transience is factored in, the job becomes extremely costly and time consuming. A high school senior hoping to graduate from a Fairfax high school may have taken a 9th grade SOL test in Virginia Beach and an 11th grade SOL test in Prince William County. Making certain that the student earned verified credits in her prior courses taken elsewhere can involve a considerable amount of double-checking. Fairfax graduates approximately

12,000 students each year, and a substantial number of them attended non-Fairfax schools at some point.

Over the past half-century, Fairfax educators have grown accustomed to keeping one eye on the horizon. Monitoring new developments has permitted the school system to avoid many of the "surprises" that have perplexed educators elsewhere and undermined their efforts to achieve educational excellence. The next section goes beyond the current challenges of external accountability systems to consider what may lie ahead for Fairfax County Public Schools.

Scanning the Horizon

When Fairfax educators are asked to discuss problems facing the school system, they display a remarkably keen awareness of emerging issues and trends. There is no tolerance for an ostrich-like approach to the future, where problems are ignored in the hope they will disappear. Fairfax educators openly discuss problems without growing forlorn and dispirited. From top-level administrators and School Board members to principals and classroom teachers, people associated with the school system tend to exude a quiet confidence that most concerns can be confronted and either reduced or eliminated. There is only one issue about which brows remain wrinkled—closing the achievement gap between black and Hispanic students, on the one hand, and white students, on the other.

For almost 4 decades, and especially during the past 20 years, closing this gap has been an important goal for Fairfax County Public Schools. There is evidence that recent programs like Success by Eight and Project Excel are boosting minority student achievement. The problem is that achievement by nonminority students also is increasing. Consequently, the "gap" is not necessarily shrinking. It is a dilemma facing not just Fairfax, but virtually every school system in the nation. Studies continue to point to different experiences at home and in the community as partial explanations for the persistence of the gap (Ogbu, 2003). Fairfax educators, along with their colleagues elsewhere, wonder, "What if?" What if, after all the interventions and all the state and federal efforts to promote accountability, the achievement gap remains? Will it have been sufficient, both politically and practically, to raise the absolute level of minority achievement, or will nothing short of narrowing the achievement gap be acceptable?

Whether or not the achievement gap can be reduced may be the most persistent and perplexing "unknown" facing Fairfax educators, but it is certainly not the only one. Contemporary school systems, especially large ones, face a number of uncertainties. For Fairfax, the sources of uncertainty include finances, local politics, and staffing.

With the new millennium has come a sustained economic downturn, rising unemployment, and unprecedented financial problems for state governments. Virginia, despite conservative fiscal policies, has not been spared. As year after year passes without hoped-for assistance from Richmond, school systems like Fairfax have been forced to beg for more local resources. Money is needed to address new federal and state mandates and keep pace with rising school enrollments. Fairfax educators feel they must run faster and faster just to stay in place. Fortunately, their *place*, at least for the present time, is at the head of the pack. Jane Strauss, a longtime School Board member and Board chair, worries that the continuation of inadequate school funding eventually could compel the school system to take resources away from middle- and high-achieving students in order to raise the bottom quartile. Such action, she warned, could have serious repercussions. By offering a variety of high-powered programs, Fairfax has been able to hold on to large numbers of high-achieving students as the county's population has grown increasingly diverse. Despite the county's large number of well-to-do residents, less than 10 percent of Fairfax's young people attend private or parochial schools (*MDR's Virginia School Directory 2001-2002*).

Accountability initiatives like NCLB compel school systems to concentrate resources on the most needy students. If top-performing students begin to abandon Fairfax schools because they believe their needs have been discounted, the future prospects for the school system darken. A public school system that serves only immigrants, the disabled, and the poor is not likely to succeed.

A second source of uncertainty, as noted in the preceding chapter, is local politics. While the politicization of educational decision making certainly predated the advent of elected School Boards, that shift has intensified partisan bickering over curriculum, school system goals, and the allocation of resources. Disagreements over money are not limited to deciding what to cut when funds shrink. When Fairfax Supervisors discovered that they finished the 2002-2003 fiscal year with an unexpected surplus of $39 million, they could not agree on how to use the money

(Bush, August 5, 2003). As the number of senior citizens and single adults grows, Fairfax educators worry that securing support for educational initiatives will become more difficult.

Maintaining a talented teaching staff, the heart of Fairfax's education empire, is another source of uncertainty. Faced with the retirements of thousands of "baby boomer" teachers and unanswered questions regarding their replacements, the school system took the unprecedented action in 2001 of creating the Work After Retirement option (Kalita, July 20, 2003). The program targeted teachers at least 55 years old with 25 or more years of service. By allowing these teachers to draw a salary as well as their Fairfax retirement benefits, Work After Retirement was designed to keep talented teachers working for Fairfax, rather than collecting local retirement benefits while teaching in a neighboring school system. The program proved to be so popular, attracting about 400 educators, that it had to be terminated early. Funds to support its continuation simply were not available.

Fairfax so far has managed to recruit more than enough qualified applicants for many positions. In 2003, for example, there were 16,000 applicants to fill 1,400 vacancies (Blakely, August 5, 2003). Problems persist, however, in certain subjects. Finding special education and mathematics teachers has been especially challenging. Fairfax officials worry that the escalating cost of local housing, highly competitive salaries in neighboring school systems, increasing numbers of challenging students, and new restrictions on teaching outside of one's certification area eventually could take a toll on their applicant pool.

Besides uncertainty, Fairfax must find ways to cope with increasing complexity. Any organization the size of Fairfax County Public Schools cannot hope to avoid completely the problems associated with organizational complexity. Keeping staff members and patrons informed about new policies and practices, for example, is a never-ending task. Monitoring school system operations to eliminate inefficiencies, reduce overlapping responsibilities, and prevent people working at cross-purposes demands constant oversight. As new programs to address shifting needs proliferate, complexity increases, demanding greater coordination and quality control. Such challenges, of course, become even more daunting in a climate of economic and political uncertainty. How Fairfax County Public Schools has been able to organize itself to address these challenges is the topic of the next chapter.

A frequent organizational by-product of uncertainty and complexity is ambiguity. Ambiguity is characterized by confusion regarding the central mission of the organization and how to achieve it. When educators feel compelled to please every special interest group in order to ensure political support and funding, the first victim may be clarity of purpose. Size also can foster ambiguity. The larger the school system, the more likely communication lines become attenuated and organizational focus blurs.

Despite rapid growth and a carnival of political distractions, Fairfax County Public Schools has not succumbed to ambiguity regarding its central mission. Credit for maintaining a focus on academic achievement belongs to leaders at every level—School Board, central office, schools, academic departments, and grade levels. Especially important has been the leadership of Fairfax's Superintendents. Under Bud Spillane, the importance of academic achievement was captured in his oft-repeated mantra, "The main thing is to keep the main thing the main thing." Dan Domenech has used highly specific district goals and individual achievement targets for every school to ensure people do not forget what they are about.

CHAPTER **6**

It Takes an Excellent School System
to Ensure Excellent Schools

When stories of educational success are told, they typically focus on individual students, exceptional teachers, and exemplary schools. Behind these successful students, teachers, and schools, however, often stands a school system committed to supporting learning and teaching. Hoy and Sweetland (2001) remind us that bureaucracies can be enabling as well as constraining. Too often derided for red tape and regulations, a well-designed and capably staffed bureaucracy can secure the resources and marshal the expertise needed to tackle problems that would daunt individual educators and schools. Previous chapters described an array of major challenges that have confronted and continue to confront Fairfax schools. Without an effective central organization, it is doubtful that these schools could have handled dramatic population growth, rapidly increasing student diversity, intensified educational politics, persistent financial uncertainty, and steady external pressure for accountability while maintaining high levels of academic achievement.

The present chapter takes a close look at the organizational structure of Fairfax County Public Schools. For those unfamiliar with the inner workings of a large school system, this chapter should foster some appreciation for the range of responsibilities required to operate a contemporary education empire. While critics often accuse educators of promoting and benefiting from "bloated" bureaucracies, the impetuses for the expansion of the Fairfax school system frequently have been external. If Fairfax County Public Schools is operated by a sizable corps of central office staff, it is probably due, as often as not, to legal requirements, government mandates, and pressures from local citizens and special interest groups for greater attention to the needs of particular groups of young people.

139

Chapter 6 opens with an overview of the organization of Fairfax County Public Schools in 1992. Subsequent organizational changes are described. Brief sketches then are provided of the various units that make up the central administration as of 2004, the stopping point for this organizational history. Particular attention is devoted to the school system's efforts to provide ongoing staff development and ensure educational accountability.

Organizing for Excellence

The organization of a *large* school system—and *The Washington Post* considers Fairfax to be the nation's largest suburban school system—is best regarded as a work in progress. School Boards and superintendents periodically tweak and tinker with organizational structure in order to improve efficiency and effectiveness, accommodate new needs and requirements, adjust to economic and political changes, and signify the commencement of a new regime. Figure 6.1 depicts the structure of FCPS in 1992. Reporting directly to Superintendent Spillane was an Associate Superintendent for Administration who oversaw planning, research, and evaluation; a Deputy Superintendent for School Operations who headed up the Area offices, Student Services and Special Education, Facilities Services, and General Services; and a Deputy Superintendent for Curriculum and Staff Development who directed Instructional Services, Vocational, Adult, and Community Education, and Communications. In addition, the offices of Community Relations; and Governmental, Business, and Industry Relations; Personnel Services; Financial Services; and Management Information Services also reported directly to the Superintendent.

Persistent budget problems in the early '90s compelled Bud Spillane to streamline his organization chart. The number of Area offices was reduced from 4 to 3, and 36 instructional positions in the Area offices were eliminated (Berry, Chamberlin, and Goodloe, 2001). Following the retirement of the school system's 2 Deputy Superintendents, their positions were eliminated and a new Deputy Superintendent role was created. Under this arrangement, all units of FCPS reported to Spillane through Alan Leis, the new Deputy Superintendent. Leis approved all personnel appointments, reviewed all major budgetary decisions, worked directly with principal and teacher groups to address concerns, oversaw

Figure 6.1
Organization Chart of Fairfax County Public Schools—1992

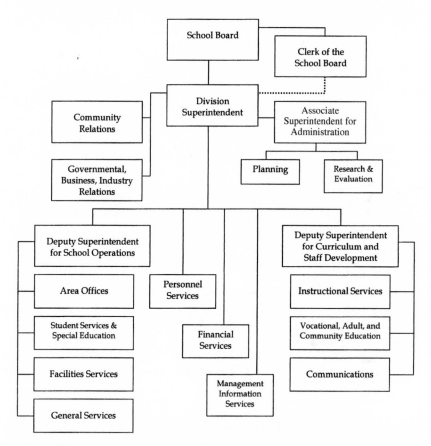

special projects, and coordinated the work of Area Superintendents and Assistant Superintendents.

When Dan Domenech arrived, the organization of the school
system consisted of the following units:[1]

Student Services and Special Education
     24 centers
     9,587 students
     130 positions

Communications
     10 positions

Facilities Services
      478.1 positions

Financial Services
      76 positions

Human Resources
      106.7 positions

General Services
      203 positions

Information Technology
      238.5 positions

Instructional Services
      3 alternative high schools
      127.5 positions   (FY 1998 Approved Budget)

Once at the helm, Domenech and his advisors began to rethink the organization of the school system. One of his first targets involved the relationships between individual schools and the central administration. Starting in the late '60s, Fairfax schools had been grouped into huge "Areas," each one comparable to a large school system. The School Board initially approved 4 Areas, each with an Area Superintendent and a substantial support staff. Spillane was forced to reduce the number of Areas from 4 to 3 in 1995 as a cost-saving measure. When Domenech arrived, the makeup of the 3 Areas was as follows:

Area I: 57 schools
             44,709 students
             25 staff positions

Area II: 56 schools
             48,603 students
             25 staff positions

Area III: 64 schools
             46,931 students
             25 staff positions   (FY 1998 Approved Budget)

In launching Project Excel to assist underperforming schools, Domenech became aware of the shortcomings of the Area arrangement (Leahy, August 3, 2000). Overlapping responsibilities between Area offices and the central administration created confusion for principals. They complained about uncertainty concerning who to contact about Project Excel business. The Superintendent sensed that the span of control for Area offices was too great to permit the kind of close monitoring and supervision expected under the new statewide accountability plan. Another problem concerned variations across the Areas. Over the years, each Area Superintendent had developed a distinct office culture and approach to handling problems. Domenech saw a need for greater operational alignment across the subunits of the school system. In place of 3 mini-empires, Domenech proposed dividing the school system into 8 Clusters. Fairfax's neighbor, Montgomery County (Maryland), already was organized around these smaller units, and Domenech admired the arrangement. Each Fairfax Cluster consisted of 3 high schools and the elementary and middle schools that fed into them. Each Cluster Director was responsible for between 20 and 30 schools, a number that permitted a more "client-centered" approach than the previous arrangement. In order for the Directors to focus more on student performance, oversight for support services such as special education, alternative education, and transportation was returned to the central administration. The 2003-2004 *Handbook* for the school system listed 5 primary responsibilities for Cluster Directors. Each Director:

- monitors, assesses, and evaluates school effectiveness to ensure that a high quality instructional program is provided for all students.

- monitors student achievement and implementation of the Program of Studies.

- directs the provision of student services.

- evaluates principals.

- responds to parental concerns that cannot be resolved at the local school.

Cluster offices were skeletal in comparison to Area offices. Each Director was directly assisted by only two individuals, a coordinator and an administrative assistant. The new cluster arrangement went into effect in August of 2000. Fairfax principals applauded the move, because it reduced the number of schools that had to compete for resources and services. The odds of securing support were better when one's Cluster contained 20 schools, than when there were 50 or more schools in an Area.

The Superintendent's desire to eliminate duplication, improve quality control, and streamline school supervision was often cited as the official justification for switching from Areas to Clusters.

One unofficial rationale ran a little differently. It held that School Board members, following the advent of elections, felt the need to be closer to their constituents. Under the Area arrangement, several Board members' jurisdictions might fall under the purview of one Area Superintendent. Board members reportedly disliked having to compete for the time and attention of an Area Superintendent in order to represent the interests of their constituents. While the new Clusters were not contiguous with the magisterial districts from which 9 of the 12 Board members were elected, they were drawn in such a way as to minimize the competition between individual Board members and allow each Board member to focus their activities more squarely on the schools that they represented.[2]

To facilitate the operation of the Clusters and provide technical support to the trio running each Cluster office, a matrix management system, modeled after those in private industry, was implemented (Berry, Chamberlin, and Goodloe, 2001). Each Cluster was assigned a team of central administration specialists representing the major departments—Human Resources, General Services, Facilities Services, Financial Services, and Student Services. Instructional Services contributed four members to each Cluster's support team—one specialist from the elementary, middle school, high school, and staff development offices. Cluster team members were prepared to respond quickly to requests from Cluster schools as well as handling divisionwide responsibilities under the direction of an Assistant Superintendent.

Just how well the Cluster arrangement will work remains to be seen. Some observers fear that it could lead to greater fragmentation, in the form of eight separate school systems with their own identities and political bases, than existed when there were only three or four Area offices. Others see a clear benefit to the Clusters. Unlike the Area offices, their small staffs convey the impression of a lean and efficient operation at a time when local resources are stretched thin.

Another change in school system organization took place following the departure of Alan Leis, the Deputy Superintendent, in 2003. Instead of one Deputy Superintendent overseeing all division operations, Domenech created two new roles—Chief Academic Officer (CAO) and Chief Operating Officer (COO). Nancy Sprague and Tom Brady were the first to serve in these capacities. This top-level division of responsibilities made it possible for one individual—the CAO—to concentrate exclusively on matters related to student performance and instructional improvement. Figure 6.2 portrays the new structure of FCPS.

The Academic Side

Under the new organizational structure, Fairfax's Chief Academic Officer heads up 3 major units—the 8 Clusters representing 241 schools and centers, Instructional Services, and Special Services. The Clusters constitute the heart of the school system, each Cluster consisting of 3 "pyramids" capped by a high school and supported by a number of elementary and middle schools. Instructional Services and Special Services are designed to provide direct assistance to schools in each Cluster. To appreciate the vast range of responsibilities involved in this process, it is necessary to examine the subunits that make up these 2 departments.

The Instructional Services Department consisted of four subunits when Nancy Sprague was hired in 1991 as Assistant Superintendent. At the time the Instructional Services Department (ISD) was regarded by some observers as a last stop for school administrators before retirement. Sprague launched a campaign to fill key positions with recognized experts in curriculum and instruction. So successful was her restaffing project that ISD specialists now are actively sought for leadership roles elsewhere in the school system. Four of eight Cluster Coordinators, two Cluster Directors, and a number of building administrators, came from the ranks of the ISD.

By 2003, the 4 units that Sprague inherited—Curriculum Services, Media Services, Instructional Technology, and Special Programs and Services—had been transformed into a 9-unit operation. The units include Instructional Technology Services, Early Childhood and Family Services, Elementary Instruction and Administrative Services, English for Speakers of Other Languages (ESOL) and Language Programs, Middle School Instruction, High School Instruction and K-12 Curriculum Services, Professional Technical Services, Adult and Community Education, and Staff Development and Training. Instructional Services touches the lives of a substantial portion of Fairfax County's residents, from preschoolers and their families to nearly 85,000 adult learners. It is the task of ISD personnel to make certain that teachers receive the curriculum materials necessary to cover Virginia's Standards of Learning, prepare high-achieving students for Advanced

Figure 6.2:
Organization Chart of Fairfax County Public Schools—2003

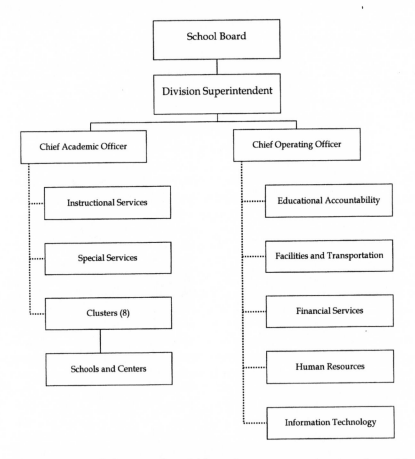

Placement and International Baccalaureate courses, and enable credit-deficient teenagers as well as adults without a diploma to pass the GED exam.

One of the most important functions under the aegis of Instructional Services is Staff Development and Training (SDT). The widely acknowledged *key* to Fairfax's success is its talented team of teachers and administrators. Making certain that these individuals stay abreast of the latest developments in their fields is the primary mission of the SDT unit and its longtime director, Sylvia Auton. She coordinates a broad range of programs designed to address the inservice education needs of various groups. The

FCPS Academy, for example, annually sponsors hundreds of courses, including college and university courses tailored to the needs of Fairfax educators and in-house courses that allow professional employees to earn recertification credits. When the school system is confronted by new challenges, whether it is a new law such as the No Child Left Behind Act or a technological innovation like graphing calculators, it is the Academy's responsibility to see that inservice education is provided in a timely manner. Most of the Academy's offerings are provided free of charge. Between its fall, spring, and summer courses, SDT annually serves almost 9,000 teachers. Many of the Academy's instructors are veteran Fairfax educators.

To promote high-quality performance from a new teacher's very first days in the school system, SDT coordinates the Great Beginnings program. Great Beginnings provides novices with ample mentoring and support, beginning in the summer prior to employment and continuing for 3 years until teachers are tenured. After-school seminars help socialize new teachers to Fairfax's unique organizational culture and familiarize them with school system policies and recommended practices. Newcomers are encouraged to bring issues and problems to the seminars. By sharing concerns, they learn that they are not alone and that the school system values an open and honest examination of work-related matters.

Another SDT initiative involves Professional Development Schools. Through cooperative arrangements with local colleges and universities, FCPS makes it possible for students in teacher preparation programs to gain valuable field experience. In addition, faculty members in the one secondary and seven elementary Professional Development Schools enjoy access to special inservice education opportunities. Other Fairfax schools are engaged in additional SDT-supported initiatives, including action research projects and the creation of professional learning communities. Many of the ideas for staff development are generated from SDT's annual survey of FCPS teachers.

Fairfax is a strong supporter of the National Board of Professional Teaching Standards (NBPTS). Besides covering the cost of taking NBPT examinations, the school system provides a $3,500 stipend to teachers who achieve board certification and agree to teach in schools with substantial numbers of at-risk students. Other board-certified teachers are guaranteed at least $1,750. As of 2004, FCPS employed approximately 110 board-certified teachers.

SDT also coordinates tuition reimbursement for educators taking courses directly from colleges and universities and a vast assortment of inservice offerings for classified employees. As extensive as are SDT's training programs, however, they represent only one component of Fairfax's enormous commitment to staff development. Every school, for example, receives an allocation so that customized staff development programs can be provided to address local needs. Other central administration units, including Human Resources, Information Technology, and Educational Accountability, are involved in various training initiatives related to their missions within the school system. Of these missions, none is more important than leadership development.

A school system as large as FCPS has an ongoing need for talented people to fill leadership roles. In 2002, for example, 90 school administrators were hired. Unwilling to leave the matter of leadership to the vicissitudes of the educational labor market, Fairfax has committed to "growing" its own leaders. Some of Fairfax's leadership development activities, such as a special Masters degree program for teacher leaders, are sponsored by SDT. Others, including LEAD, fall under the jurisdiction of the Human Resources Department and the Chief Operating Officer. LEAD is a multimillion dollar, multiyear program funded by the DeWitt Wallace-Reader's Digest Foundation. The 3 goals of LEAD are to (1) improve the professional preparation of educational leaders at all levels, (2) strengthen and diversify the pool of future leaders, and (3) create better conditions for leaders to succeed at increasing student achievement, especially for economically disadvantaged students. LEAD involves 82 Fairfax schools. At each school, selected individuals participate in horizontal and vertical learning cohorts, instructional leadership training, and the development of individual leadership plans. Administrative interns have numerous opportunities to put into practice the leadership skills they are learning. The primary focus of all training is how to improve instruction and raise student achievement. The Support Services Leadership Institute also has been created as part of LEAD, so that the leadership needs of individuals in the support services can be addressed in a systematic way.

Special Services is the third major component under the leadership of the Chief Academic Officer. Among the units that make up the Special Services Department (SSD) are the Office of Alternative School Programs, which operates a variety of alternative learning environments and coordinates character education, time-out rooms in schools, and the Suspension Intervention Program, the Office of Guidance and Student Registration Services, the Office of Psychology and Preventive Services, and the Office of Social Work and Support Services. Audiological testing, home instruction, and seminars for students involved in using alcohol, drugs, and tobacco fall under the rubric of the SSD. By far the largest unit in the SSD is the Office of Special Education. In 2000, over 21,000 students in Fairfax received special education services. The SSD operated on a budget of $12.5 million and oversaw the activities of 2,373 teachers (Boyd, Dockery, and Jones, 2003). Figure 6.3, the organization chart for the Office of Special Education, reveals the complexity of this major unit in the Fairfax bureaucracy.

The organization of special education services has been influenced by two developments—(1) the school system's commitment to inclusion and (2) the reorganization of the school system into Clusters. One consequence of these developments has been the decentralization of service delivery. Decisions regarding student eligibility for special education services used to be made at the Area Offices and the Central Office. As a result of reorganization and Superintendent Domenech's belief in more "client-centered" educational services, eligibility decisions have shifted to school-based committees (Boyd, Dockery, and Jones, 2003). This move has increased opportunities for parents and special education teachers to participate in the identification of students in need of assistance.

The reorganization of the school system into Clusters also has helped the special education staff focus on curriculum and instruction concerns related to specific grade levels. No longer must staff members try to become experts across the range of programs from preschool through 12th grade. The Office of Special Education consists of four major units (see Figure 6.3): Early Childhood/Elementary Services, Secondary Services, Integrated Technology, and Professional Development and Support Services. By assigning specialists to Cluster intervention teams, the new Office of Special Education is designed to promote greater collaboration between special education and regular education teachers.

Budget cuts have affected the organization of special education services. Besides causing a reduction in the number of teacher facilitators responsible for promoting inclusive practices, lack of funds has led to changes in Fairfax's special education centers. Center principals are being replaced by assistant principals as center leadership is shifted to the principals of elementary schools,

Figure 6.3
FCPS Special Education Organization Structure—June 2003

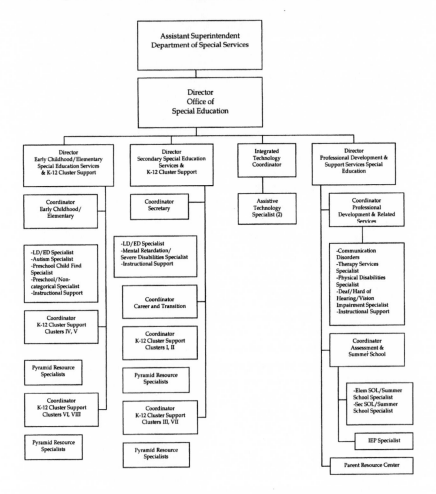

where special education centers are co-located. Future plans call for converting many centers to program status.

The Operations Side

The second component of Fairfax's new central office arrangement includes five departments that deal with school system operations. Facilities and Transportation, Financial Services, Human

Resources, Information Technology, and the newest addition, Educational Accountability, fall under the leadership of the Chief Operating Officer. The scope of operations of each department is roughly equivalent to a large business enterprise.

Facilities and Transportation, for example, operates a bus fleet of 1,500 vehicles that daily takes 110,000 students to and from school. Transportation, however, is just the beginning. The Facilities and Transportation Department also includes an enormous and award-winning Food and Nutrition Services unit, an Office of Supply Operations that is responsible for procurement, warehousing, and printing, and the Office of Safety and Security, charged with crisis management and ensuring the safety of students and staff members. Besides the routine security concerns faced by all school systems, the Office of Safety and Security in recent years has had to contend with the aftermath of the September 11, 2001, terrorist attack on the Pentagon, the Washington-area sniper attacks the following fall, and Hurricane Isabel in September of 2003.

The Facilities Services branch of the Facilities and Transportation unit handles every phase of physical plant development and operation from site acquisition to building maintenance. The Design and Construction Services office and the Facilities Planning Services office employ a small army of architects, and civil, electrical, and mechanical engineers along with planners and project managers. These individuals are responsible for determining future facilities needs, scheduling the renewal and renovation of existing facilities, and monitoring construction projects.

Seeing to the financial needs of the school system is the responsibility of the Financial Services unit. Besides ensuring that bills are paid and over 21,000 employees receive their salaries, Financial Services handles general accounting and internal auditing, insurance, and risk management. The Grants Development section searches for funding outside the tax base and state and federal allocations.

The task of ensuring that a steady flow of talented professional and support staff are available to fill Fairfax's thousands of annual openings falls to the Human Resources unit. Fairfax recruiters comb not only the United States, but foreign countries as well, in search of personnel. Between 1,500 and 2,000 teachers are hired each year. In addition, Human Resources handles employee benefits, workers' compensation, leaves of absence, investigations of employee misconduct, substance abuse testing, hiring of substitutes, and affirmative action issues. As noted earlier, Human Resources also is responsible for various staff development functions, including the LEAD project and employee orientation.

In the years since Linton Deck launched Fairfax's first concerted effort to adopt new technology, the school system has become a pacesetter in the use of technology for instructional, support, and recordkeeping activities. Much of the credit for implementing and overseeing this conversion belongs to the Information Technology unit. Everything from operating the school system's cable television channel and satellite educational network to maintaining its award-winning website is handled by IT. Its vast reach encompasses software systems support, data services of various kinds, document management, computing services, and maintenance of the school system's technology assets. One office in the IT unit is dedicated solely to anticipating and planning for future technology needs.

A cursory overview of these operational units hardly does justice to the scope and complexity of their responsibilities. Without the support provided by these departments and offices, it is doubtful that teachers on the "front lines" could achieve the impressive results of which Fairfax residents are so justifiably proud. It also should be noted that individuals in virtually every central office unit play leadership roles in their regional and national professional organizations. Fairfax places a high value on its employees achieving recognition in their chosen fields.

The newest addition to the Operations division is the Department of Educational Accountability (DEA). Perhaps no other organizational change better reflects Fairfax's commitment to continuous improvement and academic excellence. Prior to 2001, a variety of central office units were concerned with aspects of quality control, but, according to Michael Glascoe, the Assistant Superintendent who serves as the first head of the department, there was no single place where a comprehensive picture of school system performance was readily available. John English, a Cluster Director, described data as residing in "silos"—a silo for attendance data, a silo for special education data, a silo for SOL test data, and so forth. Data sources were plentiful, but it was hard to pull them together in ways that facilitated analysis and action. When Superintendent Domenech announced his commitment to data-driven decision making, it became clear that things had to change. Domenech and his School Board demanded quick access to information regarding progress on Fairfax's 10 divisionwide strategic targets. Cluster Directors pressed for a coordinated data management system that would allow them to pinpoint pockets of concern.

Creating a single department to coordinate all quality control efforts presented a variety of challenges. Over the years, various Superintendents had devolved considerable responsibility for accountability onto individual principals and school staffs. Each school, for example, had to submit an annual "school plan" to its Area Superintendent. The plans, however, often lacked measurable outcomes or benchmarks tied to school system goals. Glascoe regarded many of these plans more as annual "events" than carefully monitored processes for continuing school improvement.

Other problems stemmed from the fact that each Area Superintendent under the old structure had functioned somewhat differently, giving rise to variations in performance and program monitoring. Because many Fairfax educators identified closely with their particular school and Area, the alignment of their local efforts with systemwide initiatives could not be assumed. Nonetheless, it was difficult to justify greater centralization of quality control activities based solely on performance. Fairfax's overall record of achievement was too impressive. The "if it ain't broke, don't fix it" crowd felt they had a legitimate basis for resisting change.

The advent of the Standards of Learning, statewide high stakes tests, tough new state accreditation standards for individual schools, and the federal No Child Left Behind Act has changed everything. Pockets of low performance no longer can be hidden by a preponderance of high-achieving schools and students. Gaps in achievement between different groups of students must be monitored and narrowed. Meeting new accountability expectations demanded a much more tightly coupled set of data management and planning processes. The DEA has provided the degree of central coordination and oversight necessary to ensure that *all* Fairfax students have a reasonable opportunity to benefit from the school system's quality programs.

The DEA consists of five units—the Office of Educational Planning, the Office of Program Evaluation, the Office of Student Testing, the Office of Minority Student Achievement, and a Special Projects unit. This arrangement provides a seamless web, linking student and school performance directly to school and school system planning. The mission of the DEA is "to improve the achievement of all students and performance systemwide by promoting valid data-based decision making through student advocacy, planning, testing, and evaluation."

The accountability process begins in the Office of Educational Planning (OEP), where Fairfax's 6-year divisionwide improvement plan is prepared for the School Board and the Superintendent. The plan, which is updated annually, is based on performance data collected by DEA offices and compiled by the OEP. The OEP also facilitates school boundary and budget town meetings and assists high schools in preparing for their Southern Association of Colleges and Schools accreditation reviews.

One crucial component of Fairfax's planning process involves improving the performance of minority students. Seven of the school system's strategic targets for 2002-2004 specifically address minority students. The Office of Minority Student Achievement (OMSA) works with Cluster Directors and their school support teams "to ensure that school plans address minority student achievement issues" (Department of Educational Accountability). The OMSA also works with other departments to coordinate special programs for minority students, including Advancement Via Individual Determination (AVID), College Partnership Program, Early Identification Program, Institute for Student Achievement, QUEST, and Young Scholars. Technical support to the Minority Student Achievement Oversight Committee, which advises the School Board on minority student achievement issues, is also provided by the OMSA.

The heart of the DEA is the Office of Student Testing (OST), which provides testing materials for all county and state-mandated tests. The OST also provides training and support related to the administration of mandated tests, maintains an extensive website that provides a variety of data on the achievement of Fairfax students, and prepares in-house reports related to academic performance. The reports play a central role in Fairfax's efforts to continually improve instruction. The OST, for example, identifies domains of test questions that students frequently miss so that teachers can take corrective measures. Recently the OST has begun to focus on the preassessment of students, a move that promises to provide teachers with early indications of student deficits.

The Office of Program Evaluation (OPE) is charged with the responsibility of monitoring the array of programs intended to address the special needs of Fairfax students. Each year the Superintendent approves a program evaluation agenda to guide the work of the OPE. For each program under review, an evaluation team headed by a lead evaluator is formed. The team gathers data from program participants and other stakeholders, analyzes the data, and compiles interim and final reports to be shared first with the school system's Leadership Team and School Board and eventually with the public.

The OPE is responsible for the Quality Program Assurance System (QPAS), a signature initiative in Fairfax's commitment to educational accountability. Intended to provide the School Board with easier access to information on Fairfax's 85 special programs and services, QPAS requires every program and service to designate a manager whose duty it is to maintain basic information about the program or service. This information must include program mission and goals, number of locations or sites, groups targeted for impact, staffing, organizational structure, program budget, and program evaluation results. QPAS data allow the Superintendent and School Board to make informed decisions regarding the improvement, funding, and continuation of programs and services.

The fifth component of the DEA is the Special Projects Administration (SPA). Its duty is to provide technical support to the Assistant Superintendent in charge of the DEA and to monitor progress toward divisionwide targets. One of the primary responsibilities of the SPA is to administer and analyze the results of the school system's Client Satisfaction Survey.

One of the DEA's most impressive accomplishments to date has been the creation of the Education Decision Support Library (EDSL). Launched in July of 2002, the EDSL includes a "data warehouse" with over 17,000,000 records (as of the fall of 2003). Each year additional records covering everything from test scores to disciplinary actions will be added. Michael Glascoe refers to EDLS as "one-stop shopping for data." The EDSL provides Cluster Directors, principals, and other staff members' easy access to performance data on individual students, groupings of students based on key characteristics, students taught by a particular teacher, and individual schools. Excuses about the difficulty of retrieving data from various data bases no longer are acceptable in Fairfax.

An important component of the EDSL is Fairfax's Instructional Management System (IMS). One objective of the IMS is to provide teachers with an efficient and speedy way of identifying how individual students are progressing with Fairfax's Program of Studies (POS). The POS is aligned with Virginia's Standards of Learning, but Fairfax educators, characteristically, believe the POS is better organized and more comprehensive than the state's curriculum guidelines. As a result of the IMS, a teacher can determine which students need assistance in particular curriculum areas. The IMS includes a test-item bank to help the teacher construct sample tests for use in student assessment and a collection of research-based "best practices" for use in designing appropriate instructional interventions. An additional dimension of the IMS is parent access. An internet-based program, ParentCONNECTxp, allows parents to obtain up-to-date information on their children's progress.

One of the DEA's primary responsibilities is to share information related to progress on divisionwide targets in an annual retreat for School Board members. As a result, Fairfax School Board members have become skilled at interpreting accountability data and setting appropriate goals for improvement. Michael Glascoe believes it would be difficult to find a school system more "data-driven" than Fairfax County Public Schools.

Excellence and Efficiency

The enormous size of FCPS and the organizational infrastructure needed to support it are often the first things that attract the attention of observers. Focusing on size alone, however, can lead people to overlook the school system's concerted efforts in recent years to contain administrative costs. Fairfax County Public Schools has demonstrated that excellence and efficiency need not be strangers.

Superintendent Domenech, sensing widespread anxiety over the sputtering economy, tried to help the residents of Fairfax County appreciate the school system's efforts to save money. In his "message" accompanying the proposed budget for FY 2003 (Superintendent's Proposed Budget FY 2003), Domenech provided hard evidence of FCPS's cost-effectiveness. First he noted that Fairfax's per-pupil cost of $8,938 was less than most neighboring school systems. He went on to address the cost of managing the school system. In his words, "Administrative expenses are minimized, while resources in the classroom are maximized." Less than 1 percent of all authorized positions, according to his calculations, were devoted to nonschool-based administration. According to the Metropolitan Area Boards of Education, which monitors school systems in the vicinity of Washington, D.C., other school systems averaged 1.5 percent for nonschool-based administration. While 87 cents of every dollar spent by FCPS flowed directly to schools, the figure for similar districts, based on a survey by Educational

Research Service, was only 82 cents. The percentage of all Fairfax employees who were "school-based" rose from 87 percent in 1990 to 92 percent in 2003.

While the Superintendent willingly accepts his role as the primary promoter of the school system, he does not intend to be the sole conveyor of good news. According to Kitty Porterfield, Fairfax's Director of Communications, Domenech has launched a new initiative calling for school principals and other educational leaders to serve as good will ambassadors, telling the community why it should be proud of its schools. The Office of Community Relations has produced "fact sheets" to assist the "ambassadors" in getting the word out. As in most other areas of operation, the ambassadors' initiative demonstrates that Fairfax County Public Schools leaves nothing to chance.

CHAPTER 7

Fairfax County Public Schools and
the Future of Suburban Education

Suburban educators at the dawn of the 21st century find themselves at a crossroads. Their communities increasingly resemble cities. Population homogeneity has given way to diversity. Suburban schools enroll substantial numbers of poor, minority, and non-English-speaking students. Problems traditionally associated with cities—bumper-to-bumper traffic, steadily rising crime rates, homelessness, fiscal uncertainty, internecine politics—are becoming commonplace in the suburbs.

Will suburban school systems go the way of many urban school systems? Will capable students abandon suburban public schools in favor of private and parochial schools? Will well-to-do residents move to exurban enclaves, taking with them the resources on which suburban schools have come to rely? Will the concentration of at-risk students in suburban classrooms steadily rise, causing student achievement to spiral downward? Will talented educators quit in the face of persistent financial problems and political infighting?

Or is there a more encouraging alternative? The success of Fairfax County Public Schools in dealing with the myriad changes washing over suburban America offers hope, not just for the education of suburban students, but for the education of urban students as well. In this chapter, several reasons why FCPS should be considered an exemplary school system are reviewed. The literature is full of analyses of what makes certain schools great, but less is known about the keys to a great *school system*. The foregoing examination of the evolution of Fairfax County Public Schools offers important insights into the building blocks of systemic success. Three of these building blocks are highlighted in this chapter—a willingness to explore new responses to familiar challenges, a stable organizational culture, and an appreciation of the necessity for balance in dealing with pressures for change.

159

"The Best School System in America"

The title of this section is in quotation marks because it is not a proven fact. No widely recognized set of metrics for rating or ranking school systems presently exists. If there were such measures, however, a strong case could be made for Fairfax's placement at the top of the list.

Perhaps the most compelling justification for an accolade this lofty is the fact that the achievement of Fairfax students, based on standardized test scores, has steadily improved at the same time that the school system's percentages of poor, non- and limited-English-speaking, and special education students have risen sharply. Most school systems would be thankful if they simply were able to prevent a decline in achievement in the face of such growing diversity. Fairfax's ability to improve on its excellent track record under these conditions means that it is a great school system not only for white students and bright students, but for students of all descriptions.

The fact sheets prepared for Dan Domenech's "good news ambassadors" program provide a glimpse of Fairfax's impressive academic performance in recent years ("Just the Facts," September 2003):

- On the 2003 Scholastic Aptitude Test (SAT), FCPS students scored their highest ever (1,110), 86 points above the national average.

- More than 80 percent of all FCPS third, fifth, and eighth graders passed the math Standards of Learning (SOL) tests in 2002.

- The passing rate for the SOL English exam for third graders has rise from 68 percent (1998) to 82 percent (2002). Fifth graders have increased their pass rate for the writing exam from 80 percent (1998) to 92 percent (2002).

- 20,689 FCPS students took the Advanced Placement (AP) exams, up from 20,236, in 2002. The number of scores of three or above increased to 13,278 in 2003, up from 13,089 in 2002.

- Based on the 2003 *Newsweek* rankings, FCPS high schools are in the top 4 percent of all American high schools measured for their student participation in

Advanced Placement (AP) or International Baccalaureate (IB) examinations.

• As the 12th largest school division in the country, Fairfax County is the only large American school system to have every eligible high school on the list, with six schools ranked in the top 100 nationwide. (And this number does not include the high school that is arguably the best high school in the United States—Thomas Jefferson High School for Science and Technology. TJHSST was excluded because it does not have open enrollment.)

• All high school students in Fairfax County can choose from numerous honors, AP, and IB courses.

• Ninety-two percent of FCPS students with disabilities graduate with traditional diplomas. The remaining 8 percent earn special diplomas.

In November of 2003, the state report on the latest SOL test results provided Fairfax with additional cause for celebration (Helderman, November 11, 2003). The percentage of schools achieving full accreditation rose from 89 to 91 percent. Among the handful of schools not reaching the benchmark were special education centers and alternative high schools. Great strides had been made since the first administration of the SOL tests in the spring of 1998, when only seven Fairfax schools met state guidelines for accreditation.

Fairfax educators are proud of these accomplishments, but they are the first to admit that much remains to be done. Narrowing the achievement gap between white and black students remains at the top of the agenda. In fairness to Fairfax, however, it must be noted that the achievement gap is present in virtually every school system in the country. Furthermore, many school systems have chosen to ignore the achievement gap rather than risking public criticism and controversy. When Grogan and Sherman (2003) interviewed 15 Virginia Superintendents in the aftermath of the state's new accountability initiative, they found that only 3 division leaders were willing to publicize the achievement gap and take actions specifically designed to narrow it.

To Fairfax's credit, the school system in recent decades has openly acknowledged disparities in achievement. Fairfax educators also realize, of course, that they have to reduce disparity without reducing the quality of a Fairfax education. The parents of

Fairfax County are committed to the common good, as long as their own children receive an uncommonly good education.

By dramatically increasing access to rigorous academic programs for minority students, targeting additional resources for schools with high numbers of at-risk students, and developing a comprehensive data management system to track student progress and guide timely interventions, Fairfax has done as much as any school system—public, private, or parochial—to ensure that *all* students receive a first-rate education. Even more remarkable, in some ways, is the fact that Fairfax has achieved all this for less money per student than many school systems.

What accounts for Fairfax's remarkable accomplishments? How has this "education empire" managed to avoid the fate of so many large school systems in the United States? What lessons can be drawn from Fairfax's last half-century that might benefit other school systems, especially those in rapidly changing suburban communities?

Familiar Challenges May Not Require Familiar Responses

The story of Fairfax County Public Schools is not a fairy tale in which every hurdle is easily cleared. The road to educational excellence has been a bumpy one. The obstacles that Fairfax educators have had to negotiate, however, have certainly not been unique to Fairfax.

Consider the challenges associated with the roller-coaster ride from rapid growth to enrollment decline and then back to rapid growth. Increasing enrollments required the expansion of facilities, services, and organizational capacity. Then came a leveling off and eventual decline in enrollments. School officials had to deal with the painful and political issues of boundary changes and school closings. To make matters even more difficult, some parts of the school system continued to grow, while others were shrinking. Just as the community began to adjust to a downsized school system, enrollments picked up again.

If one word has characterized the context in which Fairfax educators have worked over the 50 years from 1954 to 2004, that word is "change." While change has been persistent, it has rarely caught the school system off-guard. Over the years, Fairfax educators have learned to scan the horizon, monitoring developing trends and anticipating their impact on education. For the most

part, the changes faced by Fairfax have fallen into predictable categories—upturns and downturns in the economy, enrollment fluc-
tuations, shifts in political power, new state and federal mandates.

Faced with a succession of familiar changes, a school system,
particularly one as large as Fairfax, might be tempted to rely on
familiar reactions. But not Fairfax County Public Schools. The
school system has remained open to new responses to predictable
challenges. Fairfax's leaders have realized that, despite having
previously faced a challenge, current circumstances may merit a
novel strategy. Dividing the school system into four large "areas"
was an effective means for decentralizing services and supervision
in the late '60s and '70s, but by the turn of the century, a new
approach, one that involved smaller subunits and streamlined
staffing, was necessary. The needs of many non-English-speakers
and special education students once were addressed effectively in
special centers. Changes in the political and economic climate,
however, led FCPS to shift from centers to school-based programs.

Receptivity to innovation has not always been the hallmark of
large school systems. Quite the opposite. Just as it is more difficult
to alter the direction of an aircraft carrier than a canoe, effecting
change in a large school system requires considerable energy and
resources. Hill (1999) found that school systems become bogged
down in politics and lose their focus. Ouchi (2003) has contended
that large school systems are more likely to be characterized by
dysfunctional bureaucracies that foster the illusion of change
while maintaining "business-as-usual." Marsh (2002) noted that
the primary obstacle to meaningful educational reform often is the
school system itself. Land (2002) explained that school systems'
capacity for making improvements could be adversely affected by
the tendency of school boards to become absorbed in financial,
legal, and constituent issues. When large school systems finally
implement changes, it is often as a last resort, when problems
have grown so great that there is no viable alternative but reform.

Fairfax rarely waits for circumstances to compel reluctant
action. Anticipating change, or what in current jargon is referred
to as being "ahead of the curve," has been highly valued for years
in the school system and the community. Programs for gifted students were introduced in the '60s, almost a decade before federal
and state government required that school systems initiate such
offerings. The same was true for special education services. Almost
a quarter century before Virginia mandated the Standards of
Learning and statewide tests aligned to the standards, Fairfax

adopted its own Program of Studies and related tests. Well before Congress passed the No Child Left Behind Act, Fairfax insisted that every school submit an annual "school achievement index report," so that progress on student achievement targets could be monitored.

Its huge size has not prevented Fairfax from taking a keen interest in exploring better ways to organize itself and achieve its central mission. Why this is so is not entirely clear, though it is likely that the community expects its school system to be in the vanguard, and Fairfax educators, for the most part, embrace this expectation. Just how responsive Fairfax has been when it comes to trying out new ideas was driven home in an interview with Nancy Sprague, the school system's first Chief Academic Officer. She reflected on some of the ways FCPS had changed between 1990, when she joined the school system, and 2003, when the interview was held.

The reforms over the 13 years from 1990 to 2003 began at kindergarten and extended through high school. To provide a more solid foundation for academic progress, for example, elementary schools with large numbers of at-risk 5- and 6-year-olds received additional resources to move from half-day to full-day kindergarten programs. "Success by Eight" was launched to ensure that every Fairfax student could read by the time they reached third grade. In 1990 the vast majority of non-English-speaking and special education students received services in separately administered centers. By 2003 most of these students were being taught in school-based programs. Project Excel made it possible for underachieving elementary schools to implement innovative ways of raising student performance. Reforms ranged from year-round schooling and extended day programs to special staffing arrangements and research-based instructional strategies.

Changes have been just as dramatic for older students. Fairfax abandoned intermediate schools in favor of middle schools during the '90s. Vocational education was transformed from a series of programs aimed primarily at students with modest academic abilities to rigorous academies with a heavy emphasis on technology and problem-solving skills. In 1990 challenging honors programs were available in some high schools, but not others. By 2003 every Fairfax high school boasted either a full Advanced Placement program or an International Baccalaureate program. Of even greater significance was the fact that these programs were open to *all* students. Another change involved Algebra I, the course that often is viewed as the biggest hurdle standing between at-risk students and college admission. In 1990 most Fairfax students took Algebra I in high school, thereby limiting their options for advanced work in mathematics. By 2003 the majority of students completed Algebra I by the end of the eighth grade. Access to the latest technology also has increased since 1990. Every Fairfax teacher in 2003 has been trained to use computers, and every school is linked electronically. Student work is now recorded in electronic gradebooks, and student progress is tracked using sophisticated information management systems.

Reviewing all of these changes, a person might think that Fairfax was a low-achieving school system in 1990. Why else would such sweeping changes be initiated? The fact is that Fairfax County Public Schools in 1990 was regarded as one of the nation's top school systems! Desperation is not the only impetus for educational change. Fairfax educators have learned that excellence is unlikely to be sustained by standing still. Openness to new ways to address familiar challenges has become a distinguishing feature of Fairfax County Public Schools. In this regard, FCPS is like the best private corporations, which use their large size to advantage while still remaining flexible and agile (Schlender, 2004).

While Fairfax keeps changing to better address the needs of its "customers," the way the school system goes about change has remained relatively consistent over the years. The change process typically begins by soliciting input from stakeholders. In many cases, outside consultants are asked to provide an independent analysis of conditions. If an area of concern is identified, a concerted effort is made to locate pertinent research and examine what other school systems are doing to address the matter. When a new approach to addressing a problem is chosen, it usually is pilot tested before being fully implemented. Pilot-testing permits kinks to be ironed out and additional feedback to be gathered. Following full implementation, reforms are evaluated periodically to make certain they continue to be effective.

The fact that changes in Fairfax are undertaken in predictable ways suggests that some aspects of the school system have remained stable over the years. These stable features help define the organizational culture of FCPS. The next section describes how this culture has become a key ingredient in the school system's success.

Successful Change Depends on Stability

At first it may seem contradictory to claim that successful change depends on a healthy dose of stability, but students of organizations long have acknowledged that it is almost impossible to effectively manage ubiquitous change. When people perceive that everything is changing, they feel threatened and overwhelmed. Resistance to reform is often their reaction. A key to Fairfax's capacity for successful change has been the stability of the school system's organizational culture.

The culture of an organization is not just an academic abstraction. Someone who spends a month in several school systems is likely to notice differences in how people talk about what they do, the examples they offer to illustrate what their systems do well, what they regard as problems, how they relate to each other, what is left unsaid, the concerns on which they choose to focus, and their daily routines and "rituals." All of these things can serve as indicators of shared norms, core values, and tacit assumptions—some of the central elements of organizational culture (Schein, 1992).

It was noted earlier in the book that Fairfax leaders make it a practice to leave nothing to chance. They insist, for example, on cultivating their future leaders instead of leaving the matter to the uncertainties of the labor market. Similar thinking led to the Great Beginnings program for teachers new to Fairfax. The organizational socialization of newcomers is simply too important to be left to teachers' lounge banter. The school system also backs up every new instructional and organizational initiative with systematic inservice training instead of relying on individuals to acquire knowledge on their own. New programs are not launched and left to fend for themselves. Every program is evaluated periodically to determine whether its goals are being achieved and if improvements or additional resources are needed. In recent years, Fairfax leaders have realized that the community is not always aware of the good work of the school system. Employees now are provided with detailed information on Fairfax's accomplishments and encouraged to become "good news ambassadors." So pervasive is the belief that nothing important should be left to chance that it constitutes a core value, a key element of the school system's culture. Not surprisingly in light of the preceding discussion, Fairfax recognizes the importance of its own culture and, therefore, makes a conscious effort to instill and reinforce values that support its mission to promote educational excellence. People do not take for granted that a robust culture automatically will sustain itself.

Great value also is placed on high expectations by Fairfax educators. It is likely, of course, that they had little choice in this matter. Fairfax County is home to a substantial number of well-educated and very successful people. These individuals let the school system know in various ways that they want the best education possible for their children. Mediocrity is not an option.

Fairfax educators do not stop with high expectations for their students, however. They expect a lot of themselves, which probably explains why conversations among Fairfax employees often involve references to long hours and job-related stress. Nearly 60 percent of Fairfax teachers hold advanced degrees. At every level, Fairfax employees routinely win awards and occupy leadership roles in their professional organizations. Many of these individuals are highly sought after as consultants by other school systems.

Because Fairfax employees tend to be highly accomplished, school system leaders at every level express great faith in their staffs. Whenever people were interviewed about the keys to Fairfax's success, they invariably began by citing the school system's cadre of fine teachers and school administrators. It is generally assumed, in fact, that if Fairfax educators cannot get the job done, it is unlikely that anyone else can. Because of their dependence on talented teachers and administrators, school system officials become very nervous when economic conditions create the possibility that Fairfax salaries will no longer be competitive.

It would be a mistake to conclude that, because Fairfax employees are held in high regard, the pressure for improvement is lacking. The culture of FCPS embraces the belief that everybody and everything can get better. Even at an outstanding school like Thomas Jefferson High School for Science and Technology, faculty members dare not rest on their laurels. Teachers across the school system have come to expect their principals to take the lead in reviewing data on school performance and working with staff members to make improvements. The school system is well-known for self-examination and self-critique. Outsiders periodically are invited to put Fairfax programs, policies, and practices under the microscope. When such inquiry reveals concerns, they are made public, the belief being that hidden problems cannot be addressed productively.

Another feature of Fairfax's culture is the tacit assumption that what is done in Fairfax County Public Schools is significant, not just locally or in Virginia, but nationally. Fairfax educators are used to being watched and held up as examples for others to emulate. Sometimes this acceptance of the limelight causes educators in other school systems to regard their Fairfax counterparts as arrogant grandstanders, but it is hard to fault educators for taking pride in their school system and themselves. In numerous interviews, individuals expressed the belief that they had a professional duty to demonstrate that a school system serving a highly diverse population can provide a rigorous education for *all* students. At a time when some school systems have been compelled to moderate expectations in the face of disappointing reports on student achievement, it is comforting to know that at least one school system has risen to the challenges of *both* diversity and educational excellence.

One cultural value to which few people made direct reference, but that was implicit in their reasoning and their actions was *balance*. So central is this belief that it is addressed as a separate *key* to Fairfax's success.

Sustaining Excellence Is a Balancing Act

There are a lot of once-great school systems in America. Because of factors under their control as well as beyond their control, they were unable to sustain educational excellence. That Fairfax has been able to do so is due in no small measure to the ability of its leaders to balance competing interests. The analogy of walking a tightrope comes to mind. If the tightrope walker ignores a shift in the wind, he risks being blown off the tightrope. A similar risk arises if he overcorrects in an effort to adjust to the change. For a half-century, Fairfax County Public Schools has managed to move forward without falling off the tightrope. In order to do so, educational leaders have become well versed in the political process. Whether they are lobbying for policy changes and resources in Richmond and Washington, dealing with efforts by the Board of Supervisors to exercise greater control over school system operations, or appealing to the public for support, Fairfax officials know how to play the game. They understand that the end result often must be judicious compromise, a balancing of competing interests.

One way in which Fairfax educators have maintained balance involves the needs of highly gifted students and students who are struggling academically. Refusing to get caught up in the excellence/equity dialectic, the school system has supported strong programs for both groups. Access to gifted education and honors courses has been expanded without eroding academic rigor. At the same time additional funding for special needs schools has allowed educators to develop programs that target at-risk students. While many special education and ESL students have been moved from centers to school-based programs, centers for gifted students have been retained. School system leaders understand that parents of bright students value the opportunities available in these carefully designed learning environments.

Balance also is apparent in Fairfax's authority structure. Over the years many important decisions have been shifted from the central administration to the schools. Site-based management has allowed principals and their staffs to customize programs and allocate resources in ways that respond to local needs. Over the same period of time, however, the school system has increased its capacity for monitoring school performance and holding principals and teachers accountable for division goals. The Excel and Success by Eight programs exemplify this balanced approach. While each school is closely watched to see that low-achieving students are improving, the schools are free to develop their own improvement plans and determine how to allocate special needs funds. The benefits of this simultaneous loosening and tightening of central control are apparent in Fairfax's record of improving performance.

A third area in which Fairfax has achieved balance concerns *choice*. Sensing increasing public demand for educational options, Fairfax has created a broad range of programmatic choices. From alternative schools to career academies, from focus schools to magnet programs, from special summer programs to year-round schools, from Advanced Placement programs to International Baccalaureate programs, the school system constitutes a market in which students can find a program to match their needs and interests. The potential risk with a market, however, is that some choices may lead to less rigorous educational experiences than other choices. To avoid this problem, Fairfax has developed high standards for all programs and appropriate policies to back up the standards. The heart of the school system's standards is the Program of Studies, which contains curriculum guidelines for all Fairfax offerings. Without programmatic variation and choice, these standards easily could lead to standardization. Fairfax leaders realize, however, that parents are not looking for identical educational experiences for their children. Blending educational options with high across-the-board standards provides a means to customize each student's schooling without sacrificing academic rigor.

Concluding Thoughts

Empires historically have overextended themselves and become targets of discontent and resistance. Whether such a fate awaits the education empire that is Fairfax County Public Schools is impossible to determine. The school system and the community so far have been able to successfully negotiate the transition from a relatively homogeneous suburb to a highly diverse metropolitan area. Some of the keys to this successful shift have been discussed—a willingness to explore new solutions to familiar challenges, a stable organizational culture characterized by self-examination and high expectations, and a belief in the importance of balancing competing interests. Exceptional leadership, an extraordinary corps of talented teachers, and citizens who actively support their schools are other crucial ingredients in Fairfax's prescription for sustained educational excellence.

It is difficult to know whether the lessons of Fairfax can be applied effectively to low-achieving school systems. Fairfax, to borrow the title from a book read by many Fairfax educators, has gone from good to great. It is one thing to improve a high-performing school system and quite another to turn around a beleaguered and failing school system. Cultures of educational excellence cannot be created overnight. Imported panaceas are not the same as home-grown reforms. Years are required to pull together thousands of talented teachers and administrators. A tradition of success nurtures itself, increasing the likelihood of future success.

While it requires decades to become a great school system, the time it takes to fall from greatness can be relatively brief. The challenges that Fairfax thus far has confronted with remarkable success—population growth and diversification, politicization of educational decision making, economic uncertainties—always have the potential to bring the school system to its knees. As a consequence, those on whom Fairfax County Public Schools depend for support cannot afford to take their school system's success for granted.

On November 4, 2003, as this book was being completed, the residents of Fairfax demonstrated once again their unwillingness to jeopardize the future of their school system. In a hotly contested election for chair of the county Board of Supervisors, Gerald E. Connolly, a Democrat, defeated Mychele B. Brickner, a Republican, and Democrats retained a 7-to-3 majority on the board. Fairfax educators breathed a sigh of relief because Brickner, who previously had served on the School Board, advocated limiting increases in property tax revenue to 5 percent a year. Such a measure, according to school officials, would have resulted in the elimination of many education programs and made it difficult for the school system to keep pace with growth.

As has occurred at other times during Fairfax's recent history, educators' relief was short-lived. A month after the Board of Supervisors election, Dan Domenech announced that he would step down in March of 2004 in order to take a position with McGraw-Hill in New York City. The news of the highly popular Superintendent's departure stunned local residents as well as school system employees. Testimonials regarding his vital leadership during trying times abounded in the aftermath of his announcement. *Washington Post* reporter S. Mitra Kalita (December 4, 2003) wrote as follows: "Domenech leaves with strong support from many members of the Fairfax school community, who moved to the wealthy county in part for the good schools. He quickly learned the politics of satisfying demanding parents, business leaders and elected officials."

The loss of high-level leadership was not limited to the Superintendent. In April of 2003, longtime Deputy Superintendent, Alan Leis, had left Fairfax to assume an Illinois superintendency. Charles Woodruff, Fairfax's Chief Financial Officer, retired in May. Then in October the school system was shocked to learn that its exceptionally capable Chief Academic Officer, Nancy Sprague, had died in her sleep from undetected heart problems. The School Board also suffered the loss of leadership, as long-time minority member Robert E. Frye opted not to run again. Two other minority board members, Ernestine Heastie and Isis Castro, also decided to retire, and a fourth minority member, Rita Thompson, did not win reelection. As a result, the governing body for one of the nation's most diverse school systems was left with a single minority member, Korean immigrant Il-ryong Moon.

The next generation of Fairfax leaders will face a variety of immediate challenges, including Virginia's continuing problems with state funding for local services, teachers' demands for salary increases, and complaints regarding badly needed school repairs. While it is too early to tell how the school system's new leaders will fare, nothing can diminish what Fairfax County Public Schools has been able to accomplish in the half-century from 1954 to 2004. The community and its schools have demonstrated that educational excellence and equity need not be mutually exclusive.

Their example brings to mind Ron Edmunds's contention that the existence of only one inner-city school in which students are performing at grade-level eliminates the excuse that it cannot be done. Fairfax's achievements have shown that factors such as huge size, rapid enrollment growth, increasing percentages of at-risk students, rising poverty, shrinking resources, and partisan politics—factors cited as excuses for declining performance by many school systems—can be managed without sacrificing the opportunity for all students to receive a quality education.

Notes

Chapter 1

1. It is interesting to note the disparities among Fairfax high schools. The percentage of graduates planning to attend college from Annandale, Falls Church, McLean, and Mt. Vernon High Schools equaled or exceeded 50 percent. The percentages for the other three high schools were much lower: Fairfax High School was 44 percent, Herndon was 18 percent, and all-black Luther Jackson High School was 41 percent.

2. A very useful history of Luther P. Jackson High School can be found in Mathelle K. Lee's "A History of Luther P. Jackson High School: A Report of a Case Study on the Development of a Black High School," a dissertation completed at the Virginia Polytechnic Institute and State University in April of 1993.

3. For an excellent history of massive resistance in Virginia, see Robert A. Pratt, *The Color of Their Skin*. Charlottesville: University Press of Virginia, 1992.

4. When E. C. Funderburk retired in 1969, he was replaced by Lawrence M. Watts. Watts died of a heart attack on June 15, 1970, before he could initiate any changes in district policies, programs, or practices.

Chapter 3

1. In 2002-2003, Fairfax County Public Schools served over 23,000 students with disabilities.

2. The high school ranking is based on the number of AP and IB tests taken by all students at a school in 2002 divided by the number of graduating seniors

Chapter 5

1. For a comprehensive history of Virginia's accountability initiative, see Daniel L. Duke and Brie Reck, "The Evolution of Educational Accountability

in the Old Dominion." In Daniel L. Duke, Margaret Grogan, and Pamela Tucker (eds.), *Educational Leadership in an Age of Accountability* (Albany: State University of New York Press, 2003), pp. 36-68.

2. Only seven Fairfax schools met state guidelines based on the first administration of the SOL tests in the spring of 1998. It should be noted, however, that the first group of students to take the SOL tests knew that their scores would not prevent them from being promoted or graduating. Initial test results were used only for norming purposes and as a general "wake-up call" for educators.

Chapter 6

1. The figures represent the staffing numbers for FY 1998.

2. The School Board consists of 12 elected members and one student representative. Of the 12 elected members, 3 are elected as "at large" members.

References

Preface

Lipton, Eric and Benning, Victoria. "With Fairfax's Celebrated Ethnic Mix, Rewards and Problems." *The Washington Post* (October 2, 1997), pp. D-1, D-5.

Introduction

Bolman, Lee G. and Deal, Terrence E. *Reframing Organizations.* Second edition. San Francisco: Jossey Bass, 1997.

Buckley, Walter. *Sociology and Modern Systems Theory.* Englewood Cliffs, NJ: Prentice-Hall, 1967.

Duke, Daniel L. *The School That Refused to Die: Continuity and Change at Thomas Jefferson High School.* Albany: State University of New York Press, 1995.

Scott, W. Richard. *Organizations: Rational, Natural, and Open Systems.* Third edition. Englewood Cliffs, NJ: Prentice-Hall, 1992.

Chapter 1

Administrative Guide for Fairfax County Schools. Fairfax County School Board. August 1, 1955.

Annual Report of the Division Superintendent, 1954-1955 through 1974-75. Fairfax County Public Schools.

Annual Report of the Superintendent of Public Instruction of the Commonwealth of Virginia, 1953-54 through 1974-75. Virginia Department of Education.

Berry, Denny; Chamberlin, Martha; and Goodloe, Amy. "Organizational Change in Fairfax County Public Schools." Unpublished paper, 2001.

Carper, Elsie. "School Bill Wins 73-18 in Senate." *The Washington Post* (April 10, 1965), p. A-1.

Commitment to Education: A Resource Manual for Planning, Programming, Budgeting, and Evaluating. Fairfax County Public Schools, Spring 1973.

Conant, James B. *The American High School Today.* New York: McGraw-Hill, 1959.

Cresap, McCormick & Paget. "Management Audit of the County School System Organization and Operation," Vol. 2. 1967.

"Decentralize School Setup, Fairfax Told." *The Washington Post* (February 15, 1968), p. F-2.

Division of Research and Testing, Fairfax County Public Schools. Information Memo #2. 1973.

"Dual School Setup Hit as Costly." *The Washington Post* (March 31, 1963), p. B-1.

Duke, Daniel L. *The School That Refused to Die.* Albany: State University of New York Press, 1995.

Duke, Daniel L., and Reck, Briand. "The Evolution of Educational Accountability in the Old Dominion." In Daniel L. Duke, Margaret Grogan, Pamela Tucker, and Walter Heinecke (eds.), *Educational Leadership in an Age of Accountability.* Albany: State University of New York Press, 2003, pp. 36-68.

Eacho, Esther MacLively. "How Fairfax County Public Schools Adopted Its Programs to Meet the Diverse Needs of Students: 1950-2000." Unpublished paper, 2001.

Education of the Gifted and Talented. Washington, DC: U.S. Government Printing Office, 1972.

Ely, J. W. Jr. *The Crisis of Conservative Virginia: The Byrd Organization and the Politics of Massive Resistance.* Knoxville: University of Tennessee Press, 1976.

"Fairfax High School Crowded." *Fairfax Herald* (September 5, 1958), p.1.

Funderburk, E. C. "Decentralization—Aimed at Improving Management Efficiency," *Virginia Journal of Education*, Vol. 62, no. 5 (January 1969), pp. 16-17.

Grant, Gerald. "Rights Act Funds Going to Fairfax." *The Washington Post* (April 7, 1965), p. B-1.

A Guide to Intergroup Education. Department of Instruction, Fairfax County Public Schools. 1965.

Handbook 2002-2003. Fairfax County Public Schools. 2003.

Helderman, Rosalind S., and Keating, Dan. "Two-thirds of Schools Meet Va. Goal." *The Washington Post* (November 8, 2002), pp. B-1, B-6.

Hinkle, Lonnie J. *A History of Public Secondary Education in Fairfax County, Virginia.* Dissertation, George Washington University, February 1971.

Jacoby, Susan. "Fairfax Schools Go Streamlined." *The Washington Post* (September 9, 1968), p. F-1.

Kheradmand, Angela. "A Cautionary Tale: A Look at the Reading and Remedial Reading Programs in the Language Arts Program in Fairfax County Schools from 1954-2002." Unpublished paper, 2002.

Lamont, Kathleen R. "Gifted Education." Unpublished paper, 2002.

Landres, Jim. "Blacks Ask School Shifts in Fairfax." *The Washington Post* (June 9, 1972), p. A-18.

Landres, Jim. "Fairfax Study Calls for Year-Round Plan for 8 Schools." *The Washington Post* (September 1, 1973), p. B-1.

Larson-Crowther, Rayna. "Head Start September 1965-August 1966. Final Report of Program under Grant No. VACAP 66-2126." Fairfax County Public Schools, 1966.

Lecos, Mary Anne Regan. *Process Evaluation in Fairfax County Public Schools: A Description and Evaluation of the Program Audit of Instruction.* Dissertation, Virginia Polytechnic Institute and State University, April 1980.

Lee, Mathelle K. *A History of Luther P. Jackson High School: A Report of a Case Study on the Development of a Black High School.* Dissertation, Virginia Polytechnic Institute and State University, April 1993.

Lessinger, Leon M. "The Powerful Notion of Accountability in Education." In Leslie H. Browder Jr. (ed.), *Emerging Patterns of Administrative Accountability.* Berkeley, CA: McCutchan, 1971, pp. 62-73.

McBee, Susanna. "26 Fairfax Negroes Ask U.S. Court to End School Segregation at Once." *The Washington Post* (August 21, 1959), p. A-1.

McClain, Jay. "The Gifts of Change: A History of Programs for Gifted and Talented Elementary Students in Fairfax County Public Schools." Unpublished paper, 2001.

Musick, Mary Lou Munsey. "Fairfax County Public Schools—The Very Best," unpublished paper, February 22, 1999.

Netherton, Nan; Sweig, Donald; Artemel, Janice; Hickin, Patricia; and Reed, Patrick. *Fairfax County, Virginia: A History*. Fairfax, VA: Fairfax County Board of Supervisors, 1978.

Pratt, Robert A. *The Color of Their Skin*. Charlottesville: University Press of Virginia, 1992.

"Proposal for the Operation of a Center for Effecting Educational Change." Fairfax County Public Schools, January 12, 1967.

"Pupil Placement Unit Rejects All Requests for School Transfers." *The Washington Post* (August 4, 1959), p. B-1.

School Board Agenda Item IV-A, School Board Minutes (February 4, 1974).

"School Board Integration Plan Arouses Controversy." *Fairfax Herald* (August 21, 1959), p. 1.

"School Plant Planning and Organization Audit." Prepared by Booz Allen & Hamilton. January 1964.

Sims, Jane. "Another Bond Vote for Fairfax Schools?" *The Washington Post* (December 19, 1974), p. A-2.

"6-2-4 Plan Adopted by School Board." *Fairfax Herald* (July 25, 1958), p.1.

"Strengthening the Fairfax County Program of Education for Gifted Children." Presented to the Fairfax County Public Schools School Board by Parents of Children in the Gifted Program. April 9, 1970.

"Superintendent's Annual Report for 1956-1957." Fairfax County Public Schools, 1957.

"Superintendent's Annual Report for 1964-1965." Fairfax County Public Schools, 1965.

Whitaker, Joseph D. "Fairfax Schools Adopt Human Rights Policy." *The Washington Post* (October 15, 1971), p. C-5.

Whitaker, Joseph D. "Parents, Teachers to Help Plan Va. Religious Holidays." *The Washington Post* (July 27, 1973), p. C-9.

Whoriskey, Peter, and Cohen, Sarah. "Immigrants Arrive from Far and Wide." *The Washington Post* (November 23, 2001), pp. B-1, B-4.

Chapter 2

Annual Reports of the Superintendent of Public Instruction of the Commonwealth of Virginia, 1973–74 through 1984–85.

"Back to Class in Fairfax." *The Washington Post* (September 11, 1980), p. Va. 16.

Bauer, Pat. "Tight Fairfax Budget Adds to Special Education Dilemma." *The Washington Post* (May 23, 1980), p. B-1.

Berry, Denny; Chamberlin, Martha; and Goodloe, Amy. "Organizational Change in Fairfax County Public Schools." Unpublished paper, 2001.

"Black Pupils Suspended." *The Washington Post* (June 30, 1979), p. C-5.

Carton, Barbara. "Fairfax Neighbors Divided." *The Washington Post* (March 14, 1985), pp. C-1, C-6.

Cohn, D'Vera. "Fairfax Pupils Again Better Than Average." *The Washington Post* (June 6, 1985), p. C-6.

Dougherty, Kerry. "Florida Educator Named by Fairfax to Head Schools." *The Washington Post* (November 20, 1979), p. C-1.

Dougherty, Kerry. "New Superintendent in Fairfax Discusses His Educational Views." *The Washington Post* (November 29, 1979), p. Va. 5.

Dougherty, Kerry. "29 Schools Eyed by Fairfax for Possible Closing." *The Washington Post* (December 1, 1979), p. C-8.

Dougherty, Kerry. "Schools: No Longer Separate But Still Unequal." *The Washington Post* (December 6, 1979), pp. Va. 1, Va. 6.

Dougherty, Kerry. "Eight Fairfax Schools May Close." *The Washington Post* (April 24, 1980), pp. C-1, C-5.

Dougherty, Kerry. "Fairfax Superintendent Begins Reorganization." *The Washington Post* (June 5, 1980), p. Va. 11.

Dougherty, Kerry. "Plan to Reorganize Fairfax Schools Criticized." *The Washington Post* (June 12, 1980), p. Va. 12.

Dougherty, Kerry. "Judge Allows School Closing in Va. To Stand." *The Washington Post* (July 24, 1980), pp. C-1, C-3.

Dougherty, Kerry. "Schools Protest Bilingual Plan." *The Washington Post* (August 14, 1980), p. Va. 2.

Eacho, Esther MacLively. "How Fairfax County Public Schools Adopted Its Programs to Meet the Diverse Needs of Students: 1950-2000." Unpublished paper, 2001.

"Fairfax Board Will Challenge Rules on Bilingual Education." *The Washington Post* (October 7, 1980), p. C-7.

Fairfax County Public Schools. *Report of the Advisory Committee on the Academic Performance of Minority Students in Fairfax County Public Schools.* Fairfax, VA: Fairfax County Public Schools, Office of Research and Evaluation, 1984.

"Fairfax County Schools Found Succeeding in Integration Plan." *The Washington Post* (February 14, 1979), p. A-2.

"Feds OK Fairfax ESL Plan." *Fairfax Journal* (January 2, 1981), p. A-2.

Feinberg, Lawrence. "Reagan Denounces Carter's Proposed Rules on Bilingual Education." *The Washington Post* (March 4, 1981), p. C-5.

Feinberg, Lawrence. "Fairfax Schools Praised." *The Washington Post* (August 7, 1982), p. B-1.

Gordon, Barbara. "Enrollment Drop: How to Cope?" *The Washington Post* (February 13, 1981), pp. A-1, A-12.

Henderson, Nell. "Businesses Boost High-Tech School." *The Washington Post* (February 5, 1985), p. C-3.

Hodge, Paul. "Fairfax Limits Secondary School Closings." *The Washington Post* (April 2, 1981), p. Va. 8.

Hodge, Paul. "Fairfax Minority Students Lag." *The Washington Post* (January 14, 1984), pp. A-1, A-22.

Kashuda, Vincent. "Every Elementary, Intermediate School Has Programs for Gifted, Talented Children." *Fairfax County Public Schools Bulletin*, Vol. 16, no. 3 (1979), pp. 2-3.

Knight, Athelia. "A Superintendent under Fire." *The Washington Post* (May 17, 1979), pp. C-1, C-7.

Lamont, Kathleen R. "Gifted Education." Unpublished paper, 2002.

Latimer, Leah Y. "Fairfax Adopts Policy on New School Boundaries." *The Washington Post* (January 27, 1984), pp. B-1, B-4.

Latimer, Leah Y. "Schools in Fairfax Cope with Influx of Foreign Pupils." *The Washington Post* (March 15, 1984), p. C-1.

Latimer, Leah Y. "Fairfax Officials Start Redrawing School Borders." *The Washington Post* (April 27, 1984), pp. C-1, C-6.

Latimer, Leah Y. "Fairfax Plans Help for Black, Hispanic Students." *The Washington Post* (May 23, 1984), pp. A-1, A-16.

Locke, Maggie. "Fairfax Officials Seek Flexibility in Law Limiting Class Size." *The Washington Post* (February 3, 1977), p. Va. 3.

Locke, Maggie. "$5.9 Million Cut in School Budget Cut Eyed by Fairfax Board." *The Washington Post* (April 6, 1978), p. Va. 9.

Locke, Maggie. "Fairfax Mulls Policy." *The Washington Post* (September 21, 1978), pp. Va. 1, Va. 10.

Locke, Maggie. "Minority Hiring Plan Is Drafted for Fairfax Schools." *The Washington Post* (March 30, 1978), pp. Va 1, Va 6.

Moore, Molly. "Fairfax's Answer to Dwindling School Aid." *The Washington Post* (November 19, 1981), p. Va. 1.

Moore, Molly. "Fairfax Cuts Its Vocational Program." *The Washington Post* (February 4, 1982), p. Va. 2.

Moore, Molly. "Board Ousted Fairfax School Chief." *The Washington Post* (June 26, 1982), p. B-1.

Moore, Molly. "Fairfax Schools: Personnel Shift Stirs Hornet's Nest." *The Washington Post* (September 29, 1982), pp. Va. 1, Va. 5.

Murphy, Caryle. "A Zero-Base School Budget for Fairfax County." *The Washington Post* (January 6, 1977), pp. Va. 1, Va. 3.

Murphy, Caryle. "Fairfax Teachers' Contract Voided by School Board." *The Washington Post* (February 17, 1977), p. Va. 1.

National Commission on Excellence in Education. *A Nation at Risk: The Imperative for Educational Reform.* Washington, DC: U.S. Government Printing Office, 1983.

Painton, Priscilla. "Fairfax Opens Search for Schools Chief." *The Washington Post* (June 14, 1984), p. C-5.

Painton, Priscilla. "Jefferson High in Fairfax Will Become Magnet." *The Washington Post* (June 29, 1984), p. C-1.

Painton, Priscilla. "Fairfax School Chief to Keep Post." *The Washington Post* (September 7, 1984), pp. C-1, C-4.

Painton, Priscilla. "Backers Fear Fairfax Bonds Threatened." *The Washington Post* (September 26, 1984), pp. C-1, C-2.

Walsh, Elsa. "Fairfax Modifies Expected Effects of U.S. Spending Cuts." *The Washington Post* (July 10, 1981), p. C-1.

Zibart, Eve. " 'Austere' Budget Proposed for Fairfax County Schools." *The Washington Post* (January 5, 1983), pp. B-1, B-4.

Zibart, Eve. "Fairfax Schools Adopt King Holiday." *The Washington Post* (May 13, 1983), p. C-3.

Chapter 3

Annual Report on the Achievement and Aspirations of Minority Students in the Fairfax County Public Schools. Fairfax County Public Schools, 1987-1988.

Baker, Peter. "Officials See Bright Side of Minority Test Scores." *The Washington Post* (December 7, 1989), p. Va. 3.

Baker, Peter. "Enrichment Program Set for 12 Fairfax Schools." *The Washington Post* (March 6, 1990), p. B-4.

Baker, Peter. "Fairfax Schools Hire Consultant on Minorities," *The Washington Post* (October 11, 1990), p. Va-1.

Baker, Peter. "School Boundaries: Where to Draw the Line, Pressured Officials to Decide Tonight." *The Washington Post* (March 7, 1991), p. Va. 1.

Baker, Peter. "Report Assails Fairfax Effort to Raise Minority Achievement." *The Washington Post* (May 16, 1991), p. C-1.

Baker, Peter. "Fairfax Schools Boost Efforts to Graduate Immigrant Students." *The Washington Post* (July 26, 1991), p. C-6.

Baker, Peter. "Clinton Sees Fairfax as Racial Model for U.S." *The Washington Post* (October 1, 1997), p. A-1.

Benning, Victoria. "Fairfax Report Shows a 3rd of Black, Latino Schoolers Lag." *The Washington Post* (August 7, 1998), p. B-6.

Benning, Victoria. "A Single Father Rich in Problems." *The Washington Post* (March 15, 2001), pp. B-1, B-4.

Branigan, William, and Cho, David. "Fairfax Homeless Rise of 25% in 4 Years Called 'Stunning.'" *The Washington Post* (March 5, 2002), pp. B-1, B-4.

Bredemeier, Kenneth. "Insulated, But Not Immune." *The Washington Post* (November 26, 2001), pp. E-1, E-3.

Brown, DeNeen L. "Spillane Submits Minority Achievement Proposals." *The Washington Post* (October 3, 1991). p. D-3.

Brown, DeNeen L. "Fairfax Sticks to Its Plan for Bailey's Magnet School." *The Washington Post* (December 6, 1991), p. C-3.

"By the Numbers." *The Washington Post* (November 24, 2002; December 8, 2002; December 15, 2002), p. C-2.

Cho, David. "County Tries Translating Its Services." *The Washington Post* (November 17, 2002), p. C-4.

Cohen, Sarah, and Cohn, D'Vera. "Racial Integration's Shifting Patterns." *The Washington Post* (April 1, 2001), pp. A-1, A-10.

Cohn, D'Vera. "Fairfax Black Students Trail Whites' Scores by 36 Points." *The Washington Post* (September 5, 1985), pp. A-1, A-12.

Cohn, D'Vera. "Fairfax Grapples with Boundaries, Merit Pay Plan." *The Washington Post* (September 3, 1987), pp. Va-1, Va-9.

Cohn, D'Vera. "Fairfax Schools Unveil Plan for Construction, Renovation." *The Washington Post* (December 15, 1987), p. D-5.

Cohn, D'Vera. "Cities and Suburbs Are Trading Places." *The Washington Post* (February 6, 2002), P. A-3.

Cohn, D'Vera, and Keating, Dan. "Area First in Nation for Black Prosperity." *The Washington Post* (October 20, 2002), pp. C-1, C-6.

Duckworth, Elizabeth. "Bailey's Elementary School for the Arts and Sciences: An Organizational History." Unpublished paper, December 1995.

"Executive Summary: ESL Task Force Report." Fairfax County Public Schools, March 9, 1993.

Fairfax County Public Schools Bulletin: August 1984; October 1984; August 1986; October 1986; August 1989; August 1990; November 1991.

Heath, Thomas. "Fairfax Board Votes a New Magnet School." *The Washington Post* (March 8, 1991), p. C-1.

Helderman, Rosalind S. "Hispanics, Blacks Do Better on SOL Tests." *The Washington Post* (October 24, 2002), pp. B-1, B-5.

Hochman, Anndee. "Fairfax: 'English and Only English.'" *The Washington Post* (July 9, 1985), p. A-8.

Kalita, S. Mitra. "Admission Bias Charges Stir Jefferson." *The Washington Post* (April 2, 2003), pp. B-1, B-4.

Kalita, S. Mitra. "Fairfax Official Laments Magnet's Scant Diversity." *The Washington Post* (August 9, 2003), pp. B-1, B-4.

Lipton, Eric. "Fairfax Targets Pockets of Poverty." *The Washington Post* (June 29, 1997), pp. A-1, A-18.

Mathews, Jay. "The 100 Best High Schools in America." *Newsweek* (May 26, 2003).

McClain, Jay. "The Gifts of Change: A History of Programs for Gifted and Talented Elementary Students in Fairfax County Public Schools." Unpublished paper, 2001.

Ogbu, John U. *Black American Students in an Affluent Suburb.* Mahwah, New Jersey: Erlbaum, 2003.

O'Harrow, Robert. "Byline." *The Washington Post* (September 2, 1993), p. Va-1.

O'Harrow, Robert. "Child Poverty Surges in Area." *The Washington Post* (May 10, 1997), pp. A-1, A-16.

Redding, Whitney. "Boundary Battle Brews in Fairfax." *The Washington Post* (November 15, 1990), pp. Va-1, Va-9.

Resource Notebook for School-based Evaluation. Fairfax County Public Schools, 1986.

Seymour, Liz. "Dearth of Minorities Alarms Va. School." *The Washington Post* (September 27, 2001), pp. B-1, B-4.

Seymour, Liz. "Parents Decry Minority Plan." *The Washington Post* (October 11, 2001), pp. B-1, B-4.

Seymour, Liz. "Diversity Plan for Jefferson Dropped." *The Washington Post* (October 18, 2001), pp. B-1, B-4.

Seymour, Liz. "Looking for an Edge into Thomas Jefferson High." *The Washington Post* (December 1, 2001), pp. B-1, B-4.

Seymour, Liz. "Jefferson High Triples Its Black, Latino Admissions." *The Washington Post* (April 9, 2002), pp. B-1, B-5.

Seymour, Liz. "Too Few Make Cut As Fairfax's Gifted." *The Washington Post* (April 28, 2002), pp. C-1, C-5.

Seymour, Liz. "English a Growing Challenge for Pupils." *The Washington Post* (June 13, 2002), Virginia Extra, pp. 4-5.

Seymour, Liz. "Minorities Swell Pool of Gifted in Fairfax." *The Washington Post* (July 3, 2002), p. B-1.

Seymour, Liz. "Jefferson High's Test-Prep Course Is Overly Popular." *The Washington Post* (October 19, 2002). pp. B-1, B-2.

"The Top High Schools," *Newsweek* (May 28, 2003). Information obtained from http://www.msnbc.com/news/912995.asp

Whoriskey, Peter. "Outside Beltway, a New World." *The Washington Post* (April 26, 2001), pp. B-1, B-4.

Whoriskey, Peter and Cohen, Sarah. "Immigrants Arrive from Far and Wide." *The Washington Post* (November 23, 2001), pp. B-1, B-4.

Chapter 4

Baker, Peter. "Absentee Rate for Teachers Falls in Fairfax." *The Washington Post* (October 24, 1988), p. D-3.

Baker, Peter. "Fairfax Teachers' Merit Raises May Shrink." *The Washington Post* (November 7, 1988), p. C-3.

Baker, Peter. "Spillane Honors Merit Pay Vow." *The Washington Post* (November 23, 1988), p. B-5.

Baker, Peter. "Spillane, Teachers Union Close Ranks." *The Washington Post* (January 19, 1989), p. Va. 2.

Baker, Peter. "Fairfax Board to Give Top Teachers 9% Bonus." *The Washington Post* (February 15, 1989), pp. A-1, A-16.

Baker, Peter. "Fairfax Teachers Say It's Lights Out for Merit Pay." *The Washington Post* (February 16, 1989), pp. D-1, D-5.

Baker, Peter. "Democrats' Rise Signals a Rocky Road for Spillane." *The Washington Post* (March 9, 1989), p. Va. 3.

Baker, Peter. "Spillane Vows No Retreat on Merit Pay Issue." *The Washington Post* (March 17, 1989), p. C-5.

Baker, Peter. "Fairfax Sex Education Plan Watered Down." *The Washington Post* (June 21, 1989), pp. C-1, C-8.

Baker, Peter. "Fairfax Overhauls Sex Education Program" *The Washington Post* (June 23, 1989), pp. C-1, C-6.

Baker, Peter. "Merit Pay Results Called 'on Target.'" *The Washington Post* (July 20, 1989), p. Va. 5.

Baker, Peter. "Fairfax Group Sues to Block Sex Education." *The Washington Post* (July 22, 1989), p. B-3.

Baker, Peter. "Fairfax's Spillane a Finalist for N.Y. School Job." *The Washington Post* (September 19, 1989), pp. B-1, B-8.

Baker, Peter. "7 Black Teachers Sue Fairfax." *The Washington Post* (October 10, 1989), pp. B-1, B-7.

Baker, Peter. "Challenge to Fairfax Sex Education Rejected." *The Washington Post* (November 11, 1989), p. B-8.

Baker, Peter. "Fairfax Sex Education Revisions Approved." *The Washington Post* (May 25, 1990), p. C-7.

Baker, Peter. "Fairfax Rethinks Program for Disadvantaged Students." *The Washington Post* (February 7, 1991), p. D-3.

Baker, Peter. "Ax Poised, Fairfax Argues the Numbers." *The Washington Post* (May 23, 1991), p. A-1.

Baker, Peter. "Merit Teachers Break Silence on Bonuses." *The Washington Post* (May 23, 1991), p. Va. 1.

Baker, Peter. "Fairfax Balances Education Budget." *The Washington Post* (May 24, 1991), p. C-1.

Baker, Peter. "Fairfax Teachers Union Sues over Frozen Salaries." *The Washington Post* (June 1, 1991), p. C-8.

Benning, Victoria. "Sex-Ed Videos Pass Review." *The Washington Post* (November 19, 1997), p. B-1.

Benning, Victoria. "Fairfax Board Votes to Show Sex Ed Video on Cable Station." *The Washington Post* (December 5, 1997), p. D-8.

Benning, Victoria. "Edited Sex Education Tapes Approved for Fairfax Schools." *The Washington Post* (December 19, 1997), p. C-5.

Branigin, William, "Va. Budget Infuriates Fairfax." *The Washington Post* (March 19, 2002), p. B-7.

Branigin, William and Seymour, Liz. "Domenech Says Budget Fails At-risk Students." *The Washington Post* (May 25, 2002), pp. B-1, B-4.

Brown, DeNeen L. "Board Is Split on Keeping Fairfax Chief." *The Washington Post* (June 4, 1992), p. B-1.

Brown, DeNeen L. "Fairfax Budget Optimism." *The Washington Post* (January 3, 1992), p. A-1.

Brown, DeNeen L. "Hundreds Protest Cuts in Fairfax School Budget." *The Washington Post* (January 28, 1992), p. B-7.

Brown, DeNeen L. "Fairfax Teacher Merit Pay Plan May Fall to Budget Ax." *The Washington Post* (February 18, 1992), p. B-1.

Brown, DeNeen L. "Merit Pay Draws New Scrutiny." *The Washington Post* (February 24, 1992), p. D-1.

Brown, DeNeen L. "Fairfax School Official Quits." *The Washington Post* (June 3, 1992), p. C-5.

Cascio, Chuck. "Playing Politics with Teachers' Pay." *The Washington Post* (March 31, 1991), p. B-8.

Cohn, D'Vera. "Rare Party-Line Vote Divides Fairfax School Board." *The Washington Post* (July 12, 1985), p. C-3.

Cohn, D'Vera. "Fairfax Urged to Revamp Plan to Select Top Teachers." *The Washington Post* (June 28, 1985), p. C-5.

Cohn, D'Vera. "Schools Moving to Merit Pay." *The Washington Post* (September 1, 1986), pp. A-1, A-4.

Cohn, D'Vera. "Fairfax School Chief Plans No New Programs." *The Washington Post* (October 22, 1986), p. B-11.

Cohn, D'Vera. "Student Progress Sought as Factor in Merit Pay Plan." *The Washington Post* (October 24, 1986), p. C-3.

Cohn, D'Vera. "Bennett Praises Fairfax Merit Pay Plan." *The Washington Post* (November 22, 1986), p. D-6.

Cohn, D'Vera. "Fairfax Vows Tougher Teacher Evaluations." *The Washington Post* (May 15, 1987), pp. A-1, A-22.

Cohn, D'Vera. "Spillane Reassures Teachers on Fairfax Merit Pay Plan." *The Washington Post* (September 1, 1987), p. B-3.

Cohn, D'Vera. "Teacher Pay-for-Performance Faces Test of Support in Fairfax." *The Washington Post* (May 31, 1988), pp. B-1, B-7.

"Fairfax County School Board to Reconsider Its Support for Survey on Sex and Drugs." *The Washington Post* (November 30, 1994), p. D-3.

"Fairfax Schools' AIDS Policy Upheld." *The Washington Post* (May 26, 1989), p. B-3.

"Fairfax to Act on Sex Education." *The Washington Post* (July 13, 1988), p. C-10.

Gamble, Cheryl. "Creationism Backlash May Have Fueled Turnout." *Education Week* (November 15, 1995), p. 12.

Heath, Thomas. "Fairfax Teachers Endorse Merit Pay." *The Washington Post* (September 30, 1988), p. C-5.

Hersch, Patricia. *A Tribe Apart*. New York: Ballantine Books, 1999.

Jones, Franklin Ross, and Bohen, Delores. "Fairfax County Public Schools: An Exemplary System." *Education*, Vol. III, no. 2 (1990), pp. 168-170.

Kalita, S. Mitra. "Fairfax Urged to Cut Special-Ed Centers." *The Washington Post* (July 9, 2003), p. B-1, B-8.

Krughoff, Alexander. "More Money or More Students?" *The Connection* (May 9-15, 2001), p. 10.

Latimer, Leah Y. "Fairfax School Board Urged to Test Master-Teacher Plan." *The Washington Post* (February 24, 1984), p. C-3.

Latimer, Leah Y. "Delay Sought in Teachers' Pay Change." *The Washington Post* (May 19, 1984), pp. B-1, B-2.

Lewis, Yvette, and Mannie, Jamila. "Behavior Disorders." Unpublished paper, 2003.

Lipton, Eric. "First School Board Election Draws a Crowd of Candidates." *The Washington Post* (June 15, 1995), p. Va. 1.

MABE [Metropolitan Area Boards of Education] Guide FY 2002. Fairfax County Public Schools, November 2001.

McDowell, Laura. "Why the Teacher Pay Plan Isn't Merited." *The Washington Post* (April 14, 1991), p. B-8.

Nelson, Rick. "Merit Pay Will Hurt." *The Washington Post* (May 12, 1987), p. A-18.

O'Harrow, Robert. "Fairfax County Schools Sex Education Program Takes a Conservative Turn." *The Washington Post* (July 15, 1994), p. C-4.

O'Harrow, Robert. "Creationism Issue Evolves in Fairfax School Election." *The Washington Post* (October 21, 1995), pp. A-1, A-16.

Raspberry, William. "A Poor Way to Eliminate Inferior Teachers." *The Washington Post* (September 10, 1986), P. A-19.

Rein, Lisa. "Agencies Must Trim $50 Million in Fairfax." *The Washington Post* (April 5, 2002), pp. B-1, B-8.

Rein, Lisa. "Worried Fairfax Parents Bombard Supervisors." *The Washington Post* (April 30, 2002), pp. B-1, B-4.

Seymour, Liz. "Domenech Proposes Bigger Budget for Schools." *The Washington Post* (January 4, 2002), pp. B-1, B-4.

Seymour, Liz. "Fairfax Mulls School Building Plan." *The Washington Post* (February 22, 2002), p. B-2.

Seymour, Liz. "Fairfax Plans Cheap Perks for Teachers." *The Washington Post* (March 21, 2002), pp. B-1, B-4.

Seymour, Liz. "Domenech Lists What Schools Could Lose." *The Washington Post* (April 6, 2002), pp. B-1, B-4.

Seymour, Liz. "Tight Times for Schools in Fairfax." *The Washington Post* (May 10, 2002), pp. B-1, B-4.

Shear, Michael D. "$2.3 Billion Budget Approved in Fairfax." *The Washington Post* (April 24, 2001), pp. B-1, B-4.

Spage, David; Wang, Grace; and Chang, Jonathan. "An Account of Fairfax County Public Schools' Employee Evaluation." Unpublished paper, August 2001.

"Supergram" (February 13, 2002). A publication for employees of FCPS.

Travers, Naomi S. "Spillane Recommends Changes in Merit Pay Plan for Teachers." *The Washington Post* (August 30, 1988), p. B-5.

Walker, R. B. "How Are Fairfax County's Public Schools Financed?" *Your Fairfax County Schools*, Vol. 2, no. 1 (November, 1960), p. 3.

Chapter 5

Bartlett, Buzz. "The Henny Penny Effect." *Education Week* (August 6, 2003), p. 48.

Benning, Victoria. "Boosting Student Achievement Is Top Goal." *The Washington Post* (September 3, 1998), pp. Va. 1, Va. 9.

Benning, Victoria. "Schools Target Higher Marks." *The Washington Post* (September 2, 1999), pp. Va. 1, Va. 4.

Benning, Victoria. "Fairfax Improves in Va. Tests." *The Washington Post* (September 15, 2000), pp. B-1, B-4.

Benning, Victoria. "Debate over SOL Tests Spawns Dueling Forums." *The Washington Post* (September 28, 2000), pp. B-1, B-4.

Blakely, Andrei. "Teacher Shortage Persists Despite Interest." *The Northern Virginia Journal* (August 5, 2003), pp. 1, 7.

Brady, Ronald C. "Can Failing Schools Be Fixed?" Washington, DC: Thomas B. Fordham Foundation, January 2003.

Bush, Drew. "Officials Wrangle with Fairfax Budget Surplus." *The Northern Virginia Journal* (August 5, 2003), p. 3.

"Celebrating Success." Fairfax, VA: Fairfax County Public Schools, 2002.

Helderman, Rosalind S. "Schools in Va. Fail Federal Standards." *The Washington Post* (September 12, 2003), pp. B-1, B-4.

Hsu, Spencer S., and O'Harrow, Robert. "Va. Lawmakers Seek Final Say over Educational Overhaul." *The Washington Post* (January 18, 1997), pp. C-1, C-8.

Kalita, S. Mitra. "Fairfax Schools' Retire-in-Place Option May End." *The Washington Post* (July 20, 2003), p. C-3.

Mathews, Jay, and Benning, Victoria. "Good Isn't Good Enough for Fairfax School System." *The Washington Post* (November 16, 1997), pp. B-1, B-4.

MDR's Virginia School Directory 2001-2002, 24th edition. Shelton, CT: Market Data Retrieval, 2001.

Ogbu, John U. *Black American Students in an Affluent Suburb.* Mahwah, NJ: Erlbaum, 2003.

Samuels, Christina A. "More Fairfax Schools Ring Bell Early." *The Washington Post* (August 21, 2001), pp. B-1, B-4.

"School Goals: Hits and Misses." *The Washington Post* (September 2, 1999), p. Va. 5.

Seymour, Liz. "Fairfax Reports Jump in SOL Scores." *The Washington Post* (September 7, 2001), pp. B-1, B-4.

Seymour, Liz. "Driven by the Ignored Child Within." *The Washington Post* (October 1, 2001), pp. A-1, A-13.

Seymour, Liz. "School Bonds Pass Easily." *The Washington Post* (November 7, 2001), pp. B-1, B-9.

Seymour, Liz. "Time Well Spent, Schools Say." *The Washington Post* (November 26, 2001), pp. A-1, A-20.

Seymour, Liz, and Helderman, Rosalind S. "Statewide Scores Improve on 25 of 28 SOL Tests." *The Washington Post* (September 20, 2001), pp. B-1, B-2.

Chapter 6

Berry, Denny; Chamberlin, Martha; and Goodloe, Amy. "Organizational Change in Fairfax County Public Schools." Unpublished paper, 2001.

Boyd, Mark; Dockery, Kim; and Jones, Erin. "Special Education and Fairfax County Public Schools: An Elementary Perspective." Unpublished paper, 2003.

Department of Educational Accountability, Fairfax County Public Schools. Powerpoint presentation, undated.

"FY 1998 Approved Budget." Fairfax County Public Schools.

Hoy, Wayne K., and Sweetland, Scott R. "Designing Better Schools: The Meaning and Measure of Enabling School Structures," *Educational Administrative Quarterly*, Vol. 37, no. 3 (August 2001), pp. 296-321.

Leahy, Michael. "Putting Oversight Closer to Schools." *The Washington Post* (August 3, 2000), pp. Va. 1, Va. 3.

"Superintendent's Proposed Budget FY 2003." Fairfax County Public Schools, 2002.

Chapter 7

Grogan, Margaret, and Sherman, Whitney H. "How Superintendents in Virginia Deal with Issues Surrounding the Black-White Test-Score Gap." In Daniel L. Duke, Margaret Grogan, Pamela D. Tucker, and Walter F. Heinecke (eds.), *Educational Leadership in an Age of Accountability*. Albany: State University of New York Press, 2003), pp. 155-180.

Helderman, Rosalind S. "78% of Va. Schools Fully Accredited after State Exams." *The Washington Post* (November 11, 2003), pp. B-1, B-7.

Hill, Paul T. "Supplying Effective Public Schools in Big Cities." Brookings Papers on Education Policy, Washington, D.C.: Brookings, 1999.

"Just the Facts." Fairfax County Public Schools, September 2003.

Kalita, S. Mitra. "Fairfax Schools Lose Domenech." *The Washington Post* (December 4, 2003), pp. A-15, A-16.

Land, Deborah. "Local School Boards under Review: Their Role and Effectiveness in Relation to Students' Academic Achievement." *Review of Educational Research*, Vol. 72, no. 2 (Summer 2002), pp. 229-278.

Marsh, Julie. "How Districts Relate to States, Schools, and Communities: A Review of Emerging Literature." In Amy M. Hightower, Michael S. Knapp, Julie A. Marsh, and Milbrey W. McLaughlin (eds.), *School Districts and Instructional Renewal*. New York: Teachers College Press, 2002, pp. 25-40.

Ouchi, William G. "Making Schools Work." *Education Week* (September 3, 2003), p. 56.

Schein, Edgar H. *Organizational Culture and Leadership*. San Francisco: Jossey-Bass, 1992.

Schlender, Brent. "The New Soul of a Wealth Machine." *Fortune* (April 5, 2004), pp. 102-110.

Index